Stallion Challenges

Stallion Challenges

FROM THE KAIMANAWA WILDERNESS TO THE SHOW ARENA

KELLY WILSON

RANDOM HOUSE
NEW ZEALAND

RANDOM HOUSE

UK | USA | Canada | Ireland | Australia
India | New Zealand | South Africa | China

Random House is an imprint of the Penguin Random House group of companies, whose
addresses can be found at global.penguinrandomhouse.com.

First published by Penguin Random House New Zealand, 2015

10 9 8 7 6 5 4 3 2 1

Cover photographs by Kelly Wilson; image of Wilson sisters, Heather Wilson

Image on pages 2–3: A wild bachelor stallion gallops across the Argo Valley in the
Kaimanawa Ranges. Image on page 7: A wild Kaimanawa foal at sunrise in the tussock
grass. Image on pages 8–9: A stallion with his mare and foal in the Kaimanawa Ranges.
Image on page 304: A wild Kaimanawa stallion trots within metres of me in the Argo Valley.
Illustration on page 5 by Rachel Henderson

Design by Sam Bunny © Penguin Random House New Zealand

Printed and bound in China through APOL, Hong Kong

A catalogue record for this book is available from the National Library of New Zealand.

ISBN 978 1 77553 834 9

eISBN 978 1 77553 835 6

penguinrandomhouse.co.nz

*This book is dedicated to the 17-year-old stallion Major KH —
you captured our hearts during your short time with us. Not
only did you inspire a new generation to love wild horses, but
you were also the inspiration for the Stallion Challenges. May
you rest in peace knowing that your legacy lives on in the lives
of countless horses that, without these challenges, would have
been destined for slaughter.*

CONTENTS

INTRODUCTION

Keeping up with the Kaimanawas

As little girls, we — Vicki, Kelly and Amanda Wilson — developed a love for horses, and over the years our passion hasn't faded. Our childhood dreams have not merely come true, but have been well and truly surpassed, from showjumping at the highest levels right through to taming wild horses and travelling the world.

We grew up with very little, only able to afford the cheapest and often most difficult of ponies. Looking back, it is hard to believe how far our love of horses has taken us, and yet, at the same time, how little has changed. We still ride bareback, although it's now for fun rather than out of financial necessity, and we still re-home and rehabilitate horses that many others wouldn't waste their time on. In contrast to our humble beginnings, we now have some of the most competitive horses in New Zealand. We travel the country during the summer months, with Vicki and Amanda competing in the Grand Prix and World Cup classes, while I simply ride and compete for fun. The knowledge and experience we have gained over the years wouldn't have been possible without the support of our parents, who share our love of horses and have always encouraged us to live our dreams.

Of the three of us, Vicki is the most singularly focused on her equestrian dreams. She is one of the most competitive riders in the country and has also competed internationally with much success. In the coming years she aims to represent New Zealand at the highest levels. Amanda also showjumps professionally at the top level, and is equally passionate about writing, filming and property development. She is currently working on her debut novel and a second documentary film. Unlike my sisters, for me showjumping is only a hobby, but over the years my work has also come to revolve around horses — I am a freelance designer and photographer for the New Zealand and international equestrian industry, and, more recently, a best-selling author. I am currently working on my third book, about our work with the American Mustangs.

While Vicki, Amanda and I each have our own individual talents, we complement each other well when we work together. Almost a decade ago we started our family business, Showtym Sport Horses, which incorporates our team of showjumpers, the Showtym Holiday Camps

TOP
Amanda and Showtym Viking, Vicki and Showtym Cadet MVNZ and
Momento (our Kaimanawa mare from the 2012 muster) and me.

BOTTOM
Vicki and Showtym Cadet MVNZ competing in the World Cup series.

Top
Riding our showjumpers at the beach.

Bottom
From the moment we first saw the Kaimanawas in the wild,
we became invested in their ongoing survival.

— 12 —

for young riders, Showtym Adult Retreats and Showtym Far Northern Adventures. Our underlying passion is to increase horse welfare on a global scale, and we are committed to starting at a grass-roots level — educating riders so that their horses have a better future.

Many of our champion showjumpers are horses that others had given up on — they were difficult, misunderstood, injured or ill-treated — and time and time again these horses have returned tenfold the effort and love we have invested in them. Most importantly, they enjoy life and thrive in the competition arena. They don't jump because they have to but because they want to, and it's proved to be a winning formula.

But perhaps one of the most rewarding aspects of our lives is our work re-homing the wild Kaimanawas; horses that would otherwise be destined for slaughter following the biennial government musters. From the moment we first saw the wild Kaimanawa herds in 2012 they have captured our hearts, and since then we have saved many wild horses.

One Kaimanawa that is particularly special to us is the 17-year-old stallion Major, whose journey to domestication was perhaps the most inspiring we've ever seen, and defied the popular belief that older stallions are too difficult to train. Although, tragically, we lost him just five months after he was mustered, his legacy lives on — in 2014, Kaimanawa Heritage Horses (KHH) launched the nation's first Kaimanawa Stallion Challenges in his memory. In its first year, this national training initiative ensured the survival of every stallion suitable for re-homing; horses that in previous years had been unfairly slaughtered due to a lack of interested people with the experience needed to save them.

In 2014 my first book, *For the Love of Horses*, was published and was instantly a best-seller; that same year, Television New Zealand (TVNZ) commissioned a television series called *Keeping up with the Kaimanawas*, which followed me and my sisters taming our wild horses from the 2014 muster. What started out as an unassuming project has catapulted us firmly onto the world stage, because of our innovative approach to raising awareness about the plight of wild horses, and has unintentionally made us public figures; sometimes it seems so far-fetched that we shake our heads in disbelief.

When we were first approached about a television series we quickly brushed it off — we didn't want to be in the public eye any more than we had to, and we didn't need the distraction of cameras following us around while we were trying to focus on taming wild horses. But the more it was discussed the more we realised that television exposure could greatly benefit the wild herds and would ensure that they had the support of the public for another generation. It was something worth considering.

Questions still remained. For example, did the benefits to the horses' long-term survival outweigh the negatives of the unwelcome invasion of our privacy? We knew that, if we agreed to do the series, our lives wouldn't be the same again, and so our decision had to be for the right reasons — first and foremost, it had to be for the good of the horses.

Tentatively we said yes, and from the moment that three-letter word was uttered our lives were altered once again; it's a turning point I'm sure we will look back and reflect on in the years to come. The crew filmed us for five solid months — from the muster right through to the first Kaimanawa Stallion Challenge, the Major Milestone, at Equidays. We'd promised the TVNZ director that there would never be a dull moment, but there was no way we could have known quite what a wild and unpredictable ride awaited us, not only with our Kaimanawas but also with our team of showjumpers.

This is the true story of the wild Kaimanawas we saved from slaughter during the 2014 muster, in particular the horses we were assigned to compete with in the nation's first Kaimanawa Stallion Challenges.

Starting deep in the Kaimanawa Ranges where it all began, we hope that you enjoy our journey and that these horses will become ambassadors for the breed, ensuring the ongoing survival of the wild herds.

Top
Vicki and Argo enjoying some quality time together in the lead up to the Stallion Challenges finals.

Bottom
Dean Whitehead, the main cameraman for the television series *Keeping up with the Kaimanawas*, filming the horses in the stallion pen at the muster.

Our first sighting of Elder, an aged grey stallion we would later save from slaughter during the 2014 muster.

CHAPTER 1

The Winter King

— July 2013

Amanda photographing
a bay stallion she saw
just metres from one of
the gates to the Waiouru
Military Training Base.

On one of the coldest days of winter in 2013 we struggled through the snow and ice to venture into the heart of the Waiouru Military Training Base, which is spread over 63,000 hectares of the Kaimanawa Ranges where the wild horses roam. A blizzard had swept through the central North Island, and snow covered much of the winter grazing where the Kaimanawas roamed.

Accompanied by an army guide, we set out in search of the wild herds, another army truck following closely behind to tow us out if the snow-drifts got too deep. Within minutes we spotted a lone horse — a bay silhouetted against the skyline — and as we drew closer we recognised his distinctive markings. He was an older stallion we had photographed in the autumn and he had made a lasting impression when he had led his sole mare and foal to within metres of us, bold and brave. Amanda had sat quietly in the grass while the stallion stood, alert but relaxed, as his foal delicately stepped forward to sniff the grass in Amanda's outstretched hand.

But today there was no chance of getting close, and the stallion's small herd was nowhere in sight. We hoped he hadn't lost them to a younger stallion and, more importantly, we prayed that he would escape the muster the following year; although not lame, he had an obvious injury to his foreleg that would mean he would be one of the horses culled, deemed unsuitable for re-homing.

Continuing on our way, we soon found another herd, although we almost missed them. Pressed in tight between shrubs and knee-deep in snow, they were seeking shelter from the wind; only the slight swish of a tail gave away their hiding spot. When they saw us, the lead mare startled, and moved to higher ground, her head low as she struggled through the deep powder, the rest of the herd following. They quickly disappeared from view and we returned to the truck, gaining altitude as we headed for the Argo Valley.

Major Hibbs, the army liaison officer for the wild Kaimanawas, was struggling to keep the truck on the road and soon it was impassable, the snow too deep to continue. The 150 horses that wintered in the Argo Valley were snowed in and could not be reached by vehicle. Disappointed, we turned around and headed south to where some of the elusive grey horses grazed.

We soon found a herd of bays standing underneath a grove of trees, only a stone's throw away from us. They watched curiously as we left the vehicle and crept closer, inching our way forward in breathless silence so they wouldn't be frightened. We were so focused on the mares that we didn't even notice the stallion until we were almost on top of him; just metres away from us stood a regal grey, peering through the shrubs, his white coat hard to see against the snow that covered the ground and clung to the branches around him. Spellbound, we paused in mid-stride, captivated by the sight of this noble stallion, mane and tail thick with dreadlocks. He remained frozen in place, unsure whether we were friend or foe.

Relaxing, he resumed eating, nibbling on the shrubs in front of him. Soon his mares wandered over to join him, and together they turned and wove between the trees into a clearing. We followed closely behind. Halting, the grey raised his head and neighed, and we watched as a bay mare trotted powerfully through the trees on the far side with three youngsters flanking her. Eight horses now stood in front of us; we watched as the new mare stepped forward to join the stallion, then together they turned and faced us. Unlike the grey, the mares and foals were plain in appearance and their broad Roman-nosed heads reminded us of warhorses long past; none more so than the lead mare, who stood shoulder to shoulder with the grey stallion, observing us with a calm and unhurried demeanour.

Obviously not feeling threatened, they soon returned to grazing; some pawed at the snow to reach the hidden tussock grass beneath, others reached up to eat the leaves from the trees. Not wanting to disturb them any longer, we returned to the truck. As we settled into our seats we saw a flash of movement to our right and, turning, watched as the grey led his herd towards us, passing close in front of the truck before disappearing around a bend in the road, snowy hoof-prints the only reminder of the scene we had just witnessed.

We listened with rapt attention to Major Hibbs as he shared stories of the grey stallion — the Winter King. For almost a decade the grey

Top
The old grey stallion in the snow made a lasting impression from the very first moment we saw him.

Bottom
Our first sighting of Honor, Elder's lead mare, whom we would
later save from slaughter during the 2014 muster.

TOP
A mare and her newborn foal the morning after the blizzard in 2013.

MIDDLE
Our first sighting of the Blaze family from Zone 15. They are easily identified by the white markings on their face and legs.

BOTTOM
This iconic chestnut stallion was mustered and branded as part of Department of Conservation (DOC) research in 1997, before being released again. He is believed to be the oldest Kaimanawa in the Ranges.

had been a favourite among the army personnel, and soldiers often got within metres of the herd before it moved off. Everyone knew the stallion by reputation, and when visitors came to the Waiouru Military Training Base they were often taken out to meet his herd since it was so tolerant of humans.

Not all the wild horses are as sociable as this grey stallion and his herd, or the bay that guards the gate into the Ranges; having spent their lives so close to the army base, these horses are used to seeing people on a daily basis and are the exceptions. The further into the Ranges you venture, the greater the horses' degree of wildness. Some of the herds in the north are actually dangerous, and we had heard stories of stallions and lead mares that had attacked people on horseback when they'd ventured too close to the Kaimanawas' territory.

As we drove on, we kept a close eye out for more horses and soon found another herd, this time predominantly grey mares led by two bay stallions. Among the herd was a wobbly newborn foal, and we were amazed that it had been born during the depths of winter and had survived such a harsh blizzard. Seeing the horses in the snow and ice only emphasised how hardy and tough the wild Kaimanawas are, and made us appreciate the extremes of life in the Ranges.

OUR SNOWY TRIP INTO THE RANGES affected us deeply, and as we made the long journey back north we felt torn, both awed by the experience and heavy at heart in equal measure. Although seeing Kaimanawas in the wild is one of our favourite things to do, it is also something we have come to dread. Most of the horses we see will eventually be mustered, and every year, as more horses become familiar to us, we know that we will be heartbroken when they are captured; especially if horses we know are drafted for slaughter.

Over the past three years we have seen wild Kaimanawas in the snow, the rain and the hottest days of summer. We've seen stallions fighting, newborn foals frolicking in the tussock, horses galloping across valleys and herds being mustered. The sight never ceases to amaze us and each time we are reminded just how much these horses have come to mean to us. One reason the horses are now so familiar is because of the stories we hear from the army officers who know the herds by name. Over the years we have come to share their extensive knowledge of the land, where each herd grazes and the dynamics of how they interact. We know that a herd of bachelors grazes in the Home Valley, that the old chestnut stallion can always be found in the Argo Basin and that the greys roam in the south near the Ammunition Range. We also know that the Blaze family is found in Zone 15, that the horses in Zone 20 are among the wildest, and that right at the back of the army land an elusive herd of flaxen chestnuts evades capture, their rare and shocking-white manes and tails well known to the soldiers.

Visit by visit, season by season, we see the changes within the herds: stallions that have lost mares, others that have gained them, and the arrival of new foals. Every time we enter the Ranges, we find horses we have never seen before; we have now photographed and filmed at least half of the 400 horses currently in the wild. It's always the stallions that leave us with lasting impressions, though, and each time it saddens us that these horses are the most likely to be slaughtered during the biennial musters because they cannot find new homes in domestication.

The publicity and support we have gained for the Kaimanawas in recent years has been huge, but at the last muster 24 stallions and 48 mares still went to the abattoir; with another muster approaching we knew that something else needed to be done. We understand the need for the musters — the smaller herd numbers are clearly improving the health of the horses and we have no quarrel with the Department of Conservation (DOC) over this. Rather, we believe that it is the public that offers the answer to the unnecessary slaughtering of healthy horses: it was now time for experienced equestrians to step up and offer these horses a home.

The foals and juveniles are much easier to domesticate and are always re-homed, but the majority of the adult horses go to slaughter because, most assuredly, befriending them isn't for the faint of heart. At one time the older horses wouldn't have been given a chance at all, but what we accomplished with our horses from the 2012 muster challenged the misconceptions. Our success with the stallions in particular had haunted some of the people who had been involved in saving the wild horses. Over the past 20 years countless stallions and mares have been slaughtered and, while heartbroken, those passionate about saving the wild horses had until then been able to sleep at night believing that the older horses were too difficult to tame; a belief that was shattered when they saw Vicki cantering her 17-year-old stallion Major down the beach bareback just weeks after he'd been captured from the wild.

We are fortunate in New Zealand to have a managed herd of only 300 wild horses, resulting in the mustering of about 170 horses every second year to maintain the numbers. Unlike America with over 80,000 and Australia with almost a million, the statistics here aren't overwhelming. As we drove home from the Waiouru Military Training Base we brainstormed, certain that we could come up with a solution to guarantee that the extra horses could be re-homed rather than culled. We knew that the biggest hurdle was finding people with the knowledge needed to tame the older horses. Professional horse trainers have little incentive to take on wild Kaimanawas; the horses are too small for adults to compete professionally, and the time and money needed to train them is extensive. When we finally arrived home in the dead of night, after eight hours of tossing ideas back and forth, we were confident that we had sketched the outline of a successful idea.

The following day we approached Kaimanawa Heritage Horses and asked if they would be interested in launching the nation's first Kaimanawa Stallion Challenges. Although tentative at first, the committee eventually fully embraced the idea. Over the next nine months the KHH team finalised details, sought out passionate sponsors and thoroughly vetted potential trainers. Equidays and the Horse of the Year show, New Zealand's largest and most prestigious equestrian events, were excited to host the challenges, which would collectively offer the nation's leading trainers $50,000 in cash and prizes in what was to become one of the most financially attractive wild horse events in the world.

CHAPTER 2

The muster—
May 2014

Steam rising from a herd of horses during the 2014 muster.

Top
Vicki jumping her stallion Showtym Levado GNZ over Ranger KH, one of our Kaimanawas
from the 2012 muster, just nine months after Ranger was mustered.

Bottom
Woodbine Legacy ST, one of the many young horses Amanda has produced
for the showjumping arena, at one of his first shows.

— 28 —

In the months leading up to the 2014 muster we were restless, keen to see what horses would be allotted to us. We had been approved for re-homing nine horses — six stallions for the challenges and three mares. Amanda and I were invited to attend the muster in our media capacity, and on the drive south we talked about the challenges.

Of the three of us, we felt sure that Vicki had the best chance of winning; she was by far the most experienced and suited to a challenge of this nature — over the years she had often trained horses to perform for the public and she was versatile in her skills. Amanda, although a talented rider and known for producing top young horses for the showjumping arena, hadn't worked with wild horses before (because she'd been filming during the previous muster), and I had never trained a wild horse without Vicki's assistance.

When working together we complemented each other, but the rules for the challenges were clear: the stallions in the competition had to be trained exclusively by their assigned trainer, and this would be an entirely new experience for Amanda and me. Privately I hoped that the Kaimanawas allotted to me would be young and small; I was unsure how I would cope with an older stallion.

During this waiting period, Amanda headed north in search of untouched horses to train — with the goal of gaining the mileage and confidence needed to work with wild stallions. She had broken in a number of horses over the years, but knew that the Kaimanawas would demand more than ever before so she prepared herself as much as possible, buying some of the most feral horses she had ever encountered; she soon won them over.

In late March, eight weeks before the muster, we brought home our three youngest Kaimanawa mares from the 2012 muster. They were now four- and five-year-olds and were ready to be started under saddle. This was to be our last practice before the muster: three sisters, three horses and a little challenge between ourselves to see who would do the best job training them. As expected, Vicki won by a long shot, and on just her second ride Remembrance was cantering over the farm. Like her sire, the late Major, the grey mare was relaxed about life; and Vicki, who had started hundreds of horses under saddle, was in her element.

Amanda and Revelation and me and Survivor soon caught up, although our horses' progress was often held up by our own caution. We lacked the extensive experience of Vicki, who was considered one of the best trainers in the country, and we liked to take things a little more slowly. On the odd occasion we allowed Vicki to bully us into trying something new, such as our first canter, and each time found that the horses were relaxed and accepting of it . . . we just needed to have a little more confidence in our own ability and in the horses' remarkable capacity to embrace change.

Shortly afterwards we flew to Queenstown with a group of friends. Once the wild horses arrived we knew there would be little time for ourselves, and we needed an adventure and some time without horses to prepare ourselves for the workload ahead of us. For eight days we sought out the most adventurous activities in the region: jet-boating, target shooting, archery, skydiving and hiking. Our absolute favourite was the canyon swing. Since all of us had skydived previously, we didn't expect to find the canyon swing challenging, but mentally it was far more terrifying than jumping out of an aeroplane — it takes a lot of willpower to jump off a cliff! As soon as we were free-falling, though, it became exhilarating, and we lined up to do it again and again. In the evenings we went out to the movies, got dressed in our warmest clothes to visit the Ice Bar, and — led by Amanda — went to a western-style bar to play pool and attempt to stay on a mechanical bucking bull.

The time passed quickly and all too soon we were on our flight home — refreshed and ready for a different sort of wild ride with the Kaimanawas.

On the eve of the muster we stayed in Ohakune. The weather wasn't promising: a front was coming through and snow was due overnight. If the wind didn't die down, there would be little chance of the muster happening early the next morning. At dawn Amanda woke to the alarm and peeked out the window to see everything covered in snow; excitedly, she shook me awake. We hurriedly dressed in thermals and snow clothes and dashed out the door to play in the swirling snow.

As expected, we soon got the call to say that the muster was delayed for another day — it was impossible for the helicopters to work in the mountains in substandard conditions, but that didn't stop us enjoying the results of the snowstorm.

Amanda and I have always been obsessed with snow, so we headed north to the Desert Road to see the tussock country painted in white; as always, we were in awe of the alpine desert landscape. By midday the weather had cleared and we returned to the army base to drive into the Ranges. It had been 10 months since we had photographed the wild Kaimanawas the winter before and we kept an eye out for horses, hoping to see some familiar faces. Close to the barracks we saw our first herd, a stallion covered in a fine layer of snow with a bird perched on his haunches, his mares grazing nearby.

Within 20 minutes the Argo Valley spread out before us, and as far as the eye could see herds were scattered over the vast tussock plains. We watched as two young colts fought, rearing and striking out in mock battle. It was sad that many of these horses would have their lives disrupted by the muster over the coming days — many would be taken from their family groups and face the certainty of either captivity or slaughter. This year, re-homing rates had increased so much that over 90 per cent of the horses had homes waiting for them. Much of this was due to the Kaimanawa Stallion Challenges — 20 stallions would be assigned to the competing trainers and most of them were also saving additional horses. Right across the country people were stepping up and offering these horses homes; although their days of freedom might be over, most of the horses from this muster would have a second chance at life.

The following morning we rose at dawn, and were relieved to see the sun peeking over the horizon, although it was still bitterly cold. By 6.30 am we were at the army base for a briefing about potential hazards, including live firing zones, ammunition and the procedures in place to ensure that the following two days would be as stress-free as possible for the 170 horses DOC were planning to muster.

Within an hour we were in convoy and heading out to the muster yards; on our way, before winding down into the Argo Valley, we saw a herd of

Top

Two stallions fighting; their herds were the first to be mustered. The chestnut on the left was assigned to me as part of the Stallion Challenges and named Anzac.

Bottom

A helicopter guides a herd of horses across the river leading up to the muster yards.

horses poised on a summit, the snowy peaks of Ruapehu and Ngauruhoe spread behind them, glistening in the early morning light. Most of the snow had melted overnight, but this high up in the mountains fresh snow still lay among the tussocks and provided a spectacular backdrop as the horses took flight.

Overhead three helicopters sped past and, realising that we had lost time watching the herd, we returned to our vehicles and continued on our way. Twenty minutes later, when we reached the media blind, two herds were already in the yards below, their final moments of freedom behind them. The helicopters had made fast progress — the herds must have been grazing just over the ridge. While the film crew, Amanda and I set up our gear, we watched two chestnut stallions fighting, rearing above the steam that rose from their herds, enraged at being trapped in such close confinement and having their mares mixed together. In the distance we could hear the helicopters at work, searching for more horses.

Herd after herd was brought in and we watched as stallions, mares and youngsters were drafted and separated into different yards. As the numbers in the stallion pen grew we kept a close eye on them, wondering which ones would become ours. Two years earlier, when we had attended the last muster, the majority of the stallions had been drafted for slaughter and it had left us disheartened; it was comforting to think that our idea for the Stallion Challenges had been successful and would now save most of these horses' lives.

The helicopter pilots were impressive to watch, and time and time again we were amazed at their level of experience and their sensitivity to working with the horses. Their ability to guide and direct the wild horses into the yards with minimal stress was a sight to behold — most of the herds calmly walked or trotted around the final bend, through the river and into the stockyards like they had been doing it their whole life. But with horses there is always an exception to the rule, and that afternoon we watched as two bachelor stallions appeared on the skyline, cantering down the hillside with a helicopter guiding them. As they neared the river they spun, doubled back and ducked under the helicopter, before galloping back the way they had come. The helicopter turned to follow, and managed to overtake them. The pilot gently turned them and got them moving back in the right direction, but again and again the horses managed to break away from the helicopter. For almost 10 minutes the pilot struggled to keep them together and moving in the right direction, but then they split up, one stallion moving to the right and the other heading left. Now that they were separated it was virtually impossible for the pilot to regain control of them, and we watched as they disappeared over the horizon towards freedom. Admitting defeat, the pilot brought the chopper back to the landing pad; we couldn't help but smile at the horses' determination to evade capture — they had well and truly earned the right to live in the wild.

A black stallion decided that captivity was not for him either, and we watched in shock as he eyed the 2-metre-high fence, then cleared it easily with his front feet and wriggled his hind legs over. Safely on the other side, he turned once to look back at his herd before galloping along the river towards the mountains — the stallion had abandoned his mares to save himself.

By this time the stallion pen already contained 20 horses; a beautiful range of chestnuts, bays, blacks and browns, but so far no grey Kaimanawas had been mustered in. Worried about the grey stallion we had seen the previous winter, I walked over to Major Hibbs to check whether they were mustering from the zone where the stallion grazed. My spirits quickly lifted when Major Hibbs said that he had found the grey's herd on neighbouring farmland, with a fence separating his herd from the targeted area. With relief I returned to photographing — the old grey stallion had been on our mind a lot over the past months, and we wanted him to remain in the wild, free to roam with his herd.

All of the horses so far had been mustered from the north, but by mid-afternoon we heard the distant sound of a helicopter from behind us. We looked out over the Argo Valley; the first herds were being mustered from the south. Almost 30 wild horses cantered out onto the plains and my heart skipped a beat when I saw that both herds had grey stallions; but, as they drew closer, it was obvious that the Winter King wasn't among them.

We watched them round the bend towards the muster yards, the helicopter quietly herding them. Even before they were through the gate, we heard the thundering of hooves in the distance and turned to see more horses galloping down across the plains, another grey stallion leading the charge. With a sinking heart I saw his thick dreadlocks flying in the wind and, behind, his unmistakable lead mare . . . I had no doubt that this was the same stallion we'd seen in the snow. He had obviously led his mares through the fence and back into the path of the helicopters. The army's favourite horse was on his last flight of freedom.

CHAPTER 3

The veteran stallions

A helicopter guides Elder and Honor as they gallop across the Argo Valley during their last flight of freedom as they approach the muster yards.

Top
During the sorting process, Elder was deemed too old and injured to re-home.
He was sentenced to slaughter before we intervened and saved him.

Bottom
A herd approaches the yards. The stallion (far right) would later be assigned
to Amanda as part of the Stallion Challenges and named Nikau.

As they came around the last bend towards the yards, the grey stallion slowed to a trot and, with a heavy heart, I watched him limp, favouring a foreleg. His lameness was evident even from a distance, shattering his chances of being one of the stallions in the challenge — there was no way the vet would miss such an obvious injury. With a sinking feeling I knew that the stallion's fate would most likely be slaughter.

Amanda came up behind me. She knew exactly what was going through my mind — like Major, the older stallion that had stolen Vicki's heart in 2012, this grey had long ago become entangled in mine. She knew me well, and as she reached me she asked if I'd try to save him if he was to be culled. With a helpless shrug I looked down at the yards where he now stood with the other stallions, separated from his herd. His life had changed forever, one way or another, but there was no point in anticipating trouble; his fate hadn't actually been decided yet.

As evening approached, I remained distracted by the grey stallion. Over 140 horses had now been mustered, and before we headed back for the night an army guide approached to offer the media an opportunity to photograph the horses up close. Thankful for the chance, I stood on the rail photographing the stallions. Even knowing that among them would be some of our challenge horses, I kept returning to the old grey. Behind me I heard movement and turned to see one of the musterers approaching. Nodding towards the grey he said the horse was well known, and that almost a decade earlier he'd been given a framed photo of him for his seventieth birthday. The horse was rumoured to be about 18 years old.

Soon Major Hibbs and a representative from KHH joined Amanda and me. As we'd feared, the vet had said that, with his obvious lameness and advanced age, the iconic grey wasn't suited to the challenge. Not wanting him to be slaughtered, they asked if we would consider saving him if the vet passed him fit to travel. With tears in my eyes I remembered how he'd been last winter, standing so proudly as he watched us; and when he'd trotted through the clearing he'd been sound, with no injuries marring his movement.

The idea of saving him had been running through my head all day and I promised to think about it overnight. Although the grey was my favourite, saving him would be an emotional decision, not a rational one. We were already saving nine horses from slaughter and didn't really have the time or the means to take on extras, especially an older stallion with an injury and no guarantee of soundness.

As soon as we got back to the hotel I called Vicki and told her everything, and to my surprise she told me to make a decision I could live with. This wouldn't have been so tough if I hadn't seen him in the snow the previous winter, and that night I got no sleep, kept awake by the knowledge that my sisters and I were his last chance — his life literally lay in our hands. By the early hours of the morning I rested a little easier, with my mind made up.

At sunrise I phoned Vicki and told her the that old boy was coming home; I even had the perfect name for him. In honour of Elder Jenks, the chairperson of KHH, I named the stallion Elder, and was excited to get back to the Ranges for the final day of mustering to see him again. Major Hibbs and KHH were relieved to hear of my decision; their favourite stallion had earned a reprieve and for that they were thankful. The vet soon passed him fit for travel and we talked about the best options to make the transition to domestication as easy as possible. After looking through photos of Elder in the snow I remembered how close he'd been to his lead mare, and pointed her out in the yard full of almost 80 mares. The vet agreed that it would be beneficial for the noble bay to remain with the stallion as one of our three assigned mares. We called her Honor.

More horses were due to be mustered that day, so we returned to the media blind to wait for the final herds to appear over the horizon. In rapid succession several herds of horses were rounded up, and by mid-morning the musterers had their quota; 163 horses were safely contained within the yards.

Their work complete, the helicopters landed, and the pilots joined us for lunch. One pilot had a worried look on his face and wanted to discuss options; one of the mares in the last herd he'd rounded up had had a newborn foal with her, but it hadn't been able to keep up with the herd. It was obviously too young to survive alone and he wanted to send out

Top
Elder's lead mare, Honor, was
assigned to us to
re-home in the hope that
the older stallion would
transition to domestication
with minimal stress.

Bottom
A helicopter herding wild horses
from the Ammunition Range.
Three of these horses —
Argo, Liberty and Promise —
were later assigned to us.

a rescue mission to bring it in safely so that it could be reunited with its mother.

Everyone wanted to ensure the foal's safety, and DOC was happy to foot the bill for the additional flying time needed to find it. An hour passed before we saw movement on the horizon. We watched as a tiny black foal came into view in the distance. The helicopter moved so slowly that I was surprised it was still in the air, and hovered just behind the foal while it walked slowly down the hill. When it approached the river, there was a muddy patch it had to cross and, exhausted, it paused. There were only a hundred metres left before the foal would be in the yards, and the helicopter drew closer to urge it forward; in protest, the foal kicked out, clipping the edge of the skids, before jumping into the bog and coming out safely on the other side. Next it navigated the river, then walked slowly up to the yards. Everyone watching sent up a cheer, and there wasn't a dry eye to be seen. The skill of the pilot was incredible, and it was one of the most heart-warming things we had ever seen. The care he took not to rush the tiny foal was moving. As it neared the other horses, a small black mare started nickering and trotted over to be reunited with the foal; settling down for a drink, the foal quickly forgot its worries. After such a show of spirit, the foal was aptly named Spirit of the Kaimanawas and sent with its mother to a home in the Hawke's Bay.

With the foal safe, the sorting process began in earnest. The stallions were the first to be drafted, and the vet took her time selecting the 20 stallions most suited to the challenges. Height, age and soundness were all taken into consideration, but it was a guessing game to some degree as the horses were totally wild and untouched, and the vet had to make fast decisions as the horses passed through the chute.

Soon 19 horses stood in the challenge pen and only a handful of stallions still remained — some were young, some very old, others injured or small — and time was taken to select the final challenge horse. One of the stallions looked younger than the rest but stood about 15 hands high — the largest of any horse mustered — while the other potentials were less than 13 hands. Finally, the vet decided that the little ponies would be too small for a fully grown man to ride if they were drawn for one of the male trainers, and the younger stallion was drafted through into the race and spray-painted with number 20.

Now that the horses were numbered, the media were allowed to see them up close and we quickly choose favourites. I loved the look of numbers 9 and 17 — one was a striking red bay stallion and the other was a beautiful chestnut with a long blond mane. I would have been happy to have drawn either of them and I hoped that luck would be on my side. There was only one horse in the pen we didn't want: number 1, a small black that tossed his head continuously and appeared to be in pain; the rest looked like lovely types.

Major Hibbs and a representative from DOC stepped forward to draw the names, and the media were allowed forward to photograph and video the draw to guarantee that there was no bias in the assignments. The first trainer drawn from the hat was Vicki; she was then drawn number 1. I glanced sideways at Amanda and saw her worried expression and knew that she also had concerns about the black stallion. I listened closely as they announced which horses were assigned to each trainer. Vicki's second horse was the young giant number 20, and I was disappointed when one of my favourite horses, number 9, was drawn to someone else. Amanda was drawn number 6; she looked at me and shrugged. I hadn't noticed a horse with a 6 spray-painted on his rump either — we would have to scope the yards out later to see which stallion had been paired with her.

Soon only five horses remained, including the chestnut with the blond mane, number 17. Amanda still had one name in the draw and I had two. We had a 60 per cent chance that he would be drawn to us and I listened with anticipation as my name was drawn out of the hat; then was disappointed when they drew number 8. Amanda's name was next and she was given number 10 . . . suddenly the odds weren't looking so promising, and indeed my second stallion was drawn as number 7. Turning to Amanda, I asked her if she'd noticed any of the horses we had just been assigned and she shook her head. These particular stallions obviously hadn't caught out attention — we weren't sure if that was a good or a bad thing.

Within moments of the draw, the first truck was loaded up; the first

24 horses for re-homing, including four of the challenge stallions, were heading to the lower North Island. We also got a glimpse of the numbered stallions and Amanda quickly found her horses: one was a plain bay and the other was a black. My two were similar-looking chestnuts — two of the smallest in the pen. Only one of the six stallions that would be joining our team had made an impression on us; the others were outshadowed by more impressive stallions and we were disappointed that we hadn't been allotted any of our favourites.

It was all hands on deck now, with the vet and the musterers working tirelessly to match horses to trucks to ensure that horses of the correct age and gender were going to the right destinations. The re-homing applications allowed several options: people could request yearlings, juveniles (which are two to three years old), adults, or mare-and-foal combos, and could also stipulate their preferred gender. Often the horses mustered wouldn't meet the preferences, so in the background KHH personnel were frantically comparing notes to see which homes were flexible; most had written a second and third preference on their application forms in case their first option wasn't available.

Amanda and I drifted over to the pen to see Elder, who was waiting with five other stallions that would be going to slaughter. Among them stood a 15-hand dapple grey that the vet had pulled from the challenge line-up because of his estimated age; the decision had surprised us because it seemed unlikely that, with his dark grey colouring, he was too old to re-home. Unlike the other colours, grey horses change with age; they are born black and become paler over the years until they are completely white. It would be very unusual for a dapple grey as dark as this stallion to be more than eight years old. Amanda watched him carefully. He was a magnificent animal and looked like a warhorse ready for battle, impressive dreads matting every strand of his mane. Turning to me, she asked whether she should try to save him and I encouraged her; since Elder was coming home with me already, it would have been hypocritical to have said no even if I'd wanted to.

She joined the vet, DOC and KHH staff to discuss options, and it was agreed that the stallion could be saved. Unfortunately, however, there

TOP
The little black stallion, number 1, was assigned to Vicki as part of the Stallion Challenges and later renamed DOC. He showed signs of pain and concerned us from the first moment we saw him at the muster.

MIDDLE
The ten wild Kaimanawas that were assigned to us during the 2014 muster ready to be loaded on the waiting stock truck.

BOTTOM
The dapple grey stallion with matted dreadlocks that Amanda later saved and named Tullock was originally allocated to the slaughter pen due to his estimated age.

was only room on our truck for 10 horses — Elder, the six challenge stallions and the three mares. KHH was struggling to match up the preferences; more young stallions had been requested than there were horses available, but none could be exchanged for the five slaughter stallions — the homes weren't experienced enough to take the larger, older stallions, which were notoriously more difficult.

Walking over to Amanda, who stood watching the dapple grey stallion, I asked her how badly she wanted to save him. She told me that if he went to slaughter she would never forget him; the impression he had made in the past few hours was imprinted on her heart. I offered her a solution: both the stallions I had been assigned for the Stallion Challenges were small and appeared to be young, and KHH had agreed that one could be re-homed to someone requesting a younger stallion, which would allow us to save the older one from slaughter. Although it would mean halving my chances in the competition, it would save an extra life. The swap was quickly made.

Only four stallions now remained in the slaughter pen, three that were injured and unsuitable for re-homing and a fourth we named Snowman, an older grey covered in battle scars. Our horses were loaded on the stock truck soon after, and I jumped in the cab to get a ride back to the army base so that we could collect our car and follow the horses north. Amanda had just flown overhead in a helicopter, filming the horses in the yards, and as soon as it landed we would be heading out.

The stock truck was swaying violently and there was a continuous banging as the stallions kicked among themselves. Three smaller stallions were in the back compartment with the mares, and in the front five larger stallions were crammed in. While we waited for Amanda I stood beside the truck and watched as two of the stallions reared in the confines of the crate. Their legs and heads were visible above the 2.4-metre-high walls of the truck as they fought, and I hoped they would settle fast.

As soon as the helicopter landed, Amanda ran down the hill towards us; sensing the urgency, she threw herself into the cab and I jumped in beside her. The truck driver, who had transported wild horses from the muster in the past, distracted us with stories from earlier musters as we navigated the rough gravel roads out of the Argo Basin.

Once again, we had wild horses to train. Although we were excited, we also knew how much work was ahead of us. Our normal lives would be put on hold for this, and we would need to spend many long hours just getting the Kaimanawas to the stage where they could be handled at even the most basic level.

Our home yards aren't sturdy or high enough to contain wild horses, so we have the horses delivered to neighbouring stockyards for the initial handling.

CHAPTER 4

Home, sweet home

The truck-and-trailer unit, loaded with wild horses, leaves the Kaimanawa Ranges.

Our horses were in the front compartment of a truck-and-trailer unit so had to travel many extra miles, detouring through the Huntly holding yards to deliver 12 juveniles before backtracking to Matamata to unload our own horses at friends' yards. The drive to our property in Northland was too far for the horses to go in one day, so Vicki had driven south to help us manage the wild horses overnight. Amanda and I arrived well before the horses; together with Vicki we laid out fresh hay and water, and as darkness set in we waited impatiently for the horses to arrive.

During the wait, we got a call from our friend Simone from KHH. The final horses had been sorted at the muster yard and just 15 had gone to slaughter, down from 72 the previous muster and hundreds in earlier years. She herself had saved Snowman, which meant that every stallion suitable for re-homing had been saved — the first time this had happened in over 20 years of mustering. The Kaimanawa Stallion Challenges had changed the horses' fate entirely.

Of the 12 mares that had gone to slaughter, about eight could have been re-homed if there had been enough demand, and we hoped that more mares would be considered for re-homing in the future. Around the country 147 horses were currently in transit, being distributed to new homes throughout the North Island.

By the time our horses arrived at 9 pm they had been on the truck for seven hours, and they were all a little shell-shocked. One by one they walked shakily down the ramp into the stockyards. The chestnut mare stopped and stood in the gateway like a statue; Vicki approached to encourage her to move and the mare wasn't even startled by her close proximity, standing still while Vicki reached up to scratch her head. Slowly the mare stepped forward to join the other horses and Vicki swung up onto the roof to open the middle partition and let out the big stallions.

They were squashed in tightly, and it took a while before they realised the gate was open. After some encouragement the first horse slowly moved forward, walking down the ramp and into the waiting yards; the others soon followed. Elder was visibly worried and looked the worse for wear, so we drafted him into a smaller yard and put his mare in with him for the night. The rest of the horses we split up into groups of two or three, and Vicki moved among them with a flashlight, checking for any injuries and getting a feel for the horses that had come home with us. Amanda and I were a little worried about leaving the horses unattended for the night, but Vicki was confident that they were too exhausted to do anything other than sleep so we headed up to the house to get some much-needed rest ourselves.

We woke at sunrise and hurried down to the stockyards, and in the light of day Vicki was even more impressed with the horses — the three mares were all stunning types with beautiful heads and lovely colouring, and were all full-sized ponies, and the stallions were nice types, too. As we looked the horses over we discussed names for them. Vicki named her large stallion Argo after the valley they were mustered from, and the black one she called DOC in honour of the men from the Department of Conservation who assisted in the musters. Amanda named her larger bay stallion Nikau after one of the companies that had sponsored our work with the wild horses, and her black one was called Hoff after one of the army officers who always wore black; we'd jokingly told him a year earlier that if we got a black stallion we'd name it after him, and so we did. My little chestnut was even smaller up close, but he had more spirit and fight than any of the others so I named him Anzac — a fitting name for a horse that had grown up on army land. Up close, Elder and Honor suited the names we'd given them the day before, which left just three horses to name. The dapple grey we called Tullock after the head musterer who had been responsible for initiating the musters 20 years earlier when the government had first proposed culling the horses from the air, and the grey mare we named Liberty (Libby for short), but nothing felt right for the chestnut mare so we left her unnamed; the right name would come to us eventually.

We loaded the horses at 8 am. They still had a long drive to go and we knew that the journey would take a lot out of them, but there was little we could do — the sooner they got home, the less traumatic it would be for them. Six hours later we pulled up at our neighbours' stockyards and were relieved to see Mum and Kirsty, one of the girls who works with us, waiting. The yards had been well prepared — we had spent a lot of time planning how best to manage the stockyards, and had lined the floors with weed mat and then spread hay thickly over it to ensure that the horses' hooves wouldn't be damaged.

The horses in the first compartment rushed off and we quickly sorted the mares and stallions into separate pens. The larger stallions in the front were getting restless, and as soon as the others were sorted we opened the partition and let the big boys out. The first four looked dazed as they walked down the ramp, but Elder stood in the corner with his head lowered, refusing to move. With some encouragement he finally turned, and as he stepped out of the truck and into the light everyone was concerned — his white coat was streaked with blood from being bitten by the other stallions. He looked a shadow of his former self, sunken in and depressed. Stiffly he limped down the ramp and into an open yard to join Honor, and I felt guilty for making such an old stallion do the trip north. In despair I wondered just how well he would adjust to all the changes ahead of him; perhaps slaughter would have been the kinder option after all. Moving off, we left him to settle while we introduced Mum to the rest of the horses.

When we got to DOC's yard he was standing in the corner tossing his head and sucking in wind, which is often a sign of pain. Vicki looked at us in dismay; it wasn't a promising start to be working with a wild horse that had pre-existing behavioural issues. Hoping that her other one was a more promising candidate for the competition, she moved away to watch Argo. Glancing over to us, she shook her head and laughed at the irony of it: Argo was obviously younger than the rest and, although Vicki was the most experienced of the three of us, both of her horses seemed ill-suited to an intensive competition.

Amanda's horses, on the other hand, appeared quite promising: the black was bold and beautiful and looked like everyone's dream stallion, and Nikau was a very athletic type. On first impression Vicki thought he would be the most promising — he had the conformation to make a top competition prospect and she was confident he'd do well in the Stallion Challenges.

When we got to Anzac's yard, we paused and watched quietly. My little

TOP
When he was first unloaded off the stock truck, Elder was bloody and withdrawn.

BOTTOM
Tullock was the first of the Kaimanawas to eat from our hands,
just hours after arriving in the stock truck.

chestnut was trying to pick a fight with Tullock and had more attitude than any of the other stallions. Laughing again, Vicki looked at me and said I should have been careful what I wished for . . . I'd asked for a small stallion and I'd got exactly that — complete with 'small man syndrome'. Shaking her head in amusement, Vicki moved off to look at the rest of the horses, all of which had lost condition greatly since they were mustered. Once they were settled with hay and water, we headed home to sort through photos and find images of them in the wild so that Vicki could appreciate how magnificent they had looked only days earlier; we also wanted to work out which herds they had belonged to and whether they had been mustered from the north or the south side of the Ranges.

THE FOLLOWING MORNING WE BEGAN WORKING with the horses — we were well into the heart of winter, and the sooner we got the horses handled and leading safely, the sooner we could get them home to covered yards. Vicki and the girls began working with Liberty and the chestnut mare, and they quickly settled and stood quietly to be haltered. Argo was also easy, and was the first of our Stallion Challenges horses to be touched; Vicki was very proud of him. Next, Honor and Elder were brought forward and handled for the first time. Once they were in the race I approached the grey stallion; talking quietly, I laid a hand lightly on his back. Shifting nervously, he swung his head around to look at me, standing on the boardwalk above him, then soon relaxed. Beside me, Vicki worked with Honor, and once both horses were comfortable with our hands stroking their backs and necks we let them return to their yard; they were done for the day.

The Kaimanawas are some of the wildest horses on the planet, but they also have a remarkable ability to adapt well to domestication. Part of this is because they have never had a negative experience with humans. We love that we can start with a completely blank canvas. The horses' decision to trust or fear humans comes down to their interactions with us, especially their first impressions, so we are careful to minimise any negative experiences and earn their confidence. Wild horses have a fight-or-flight response in stressful situations, so in their handling we avoid all conflict. Instead we concentrate on winning their friendship and trust. We don't demand that they submit to us, or rope them so they can't move; nor do we chase them around a pen until they are so exhausted that they stand to be approached. Rather, we take as much time as they need, aiming to give them positive handling experiences. One of the most effective ways of gaining their trust is through a hands-on approach, and we have found that working the horses in the stockyard race for the first couple of days offers a safe environment that allows us to start handling them straight away. The positive time we are able to spend with the horses helps them to relax; the horses quickly realise that we are not there to hurt them, and their whole demeanour softens — they no longer fear us or the changes ahead of them, but begin to embrace everything asked of them.

With most of the horses, progress is consistent and within days they can be led and touched. The sooner they reach this milestone, the better it is for their emotional and physical well-being because then they can be trusted to leave the depressing confines of the stockyards and start having enjoyable adventures. Like people, however, every horse is different; and at times taming wild horses — especially the older ones — has the potential to be dangerous. That morning, when we'd been feeding out hay, we noticed blood on Hoff's head, so Amanda entered his yard to get a closer look while Vicki and I watched from the fence, hoping to be able to see the extent of the damage. The black stallion was very curious and boldly approached Amanda; in surprise she glanced up at Vicki and me, a smile spreading across her face. Slowly, Amanda held a hand out to him to say hello, and pricking his ears forward he stepped towards her and stretched out his muzzle to sniff her.

Vicki and I watched in disbelief: his confidence and inquisitive nature were unusual for a wild stallion, and we waited in anticipation, sure we were about to witness something remarkable. Turning away, Amanda grabbed a handful of grass and offered it to Hoff — but, in contrast to his behaviour only seconds before, the stallion leapt forward, baring his teeth and lunging at Amanda with vicious intent. Terrified, she rushed backwards, grabbing the rails to frantically scale the 1.8-metre fence as the horse's teeth snapped shut, narrowly missing her. Hyperventilating,

TOP
Hoff was unloaded off the stock truck with a puncture wound on his head and his skull exposed.

BOTTOM
When Argo first arrived, he was nothing special to look at and, due to his age, Vicki didn't have high hopes for him in the Stallion Challenges.

Amanda looked down at the horse as it eyed her, pawing at the ground, and she held tight to the rails, keeping out of his reach.

Her voice shaking, she joked that if the horse had been on the McDonald's menu he would have been called a Hoff Burger, because at that moment he looked like a raging Angus bull. Neither of us envied Amanda at all; it was a timely reminder that these horses were difficult and had the potential to be very dangerous. Unwilling to enter Hoff's yard again, we opened the gate and directed him into the race so that Amanda could work him from the safety of the boardwalk — he had many changes ahead of him and needed to learn that humans were not an enemy.

Up close, the trauma to his head was even worse than we'd expected; his skull was exposed and the wound was infected. It was important to get him handled enough so we could treat him over the next few days — much of his aggressive behaviour was probably because he was in pain. For the next hour Amanda worked gently with the angry horse, but never made a breakthrough. He was averse to being touched and tried to break out of the yard every time she drew near; there was no way we could get close enough to safely halter him or treat his wound.

Once Hoff was released back into the larger yard, Amanda went in search of long grass and stood with Tullock and Nikau, holding the grass out for them to eat. This is generally a pointless task so early after a muster — it takes a while for the horses to settle and feel safe enough to approach people — but Tullock surprised us all by stepping forward and calmly tugging the grass from Amanda's outstretched hand. Her face spread into a huge smile — it would have been a crime to send such a gentle and inquisitive horse to slaughter, and she was so glad she'd been able to save him.

Over the fence I was spending some quiet time with my challenge stallion Anzac, but he wasn't as receptive as Tullock. In fact, he wasn't interested in me at all, and I was a little disappointed; he looked like a troublemaker and prowled around his yard, striking out and trying to bite the other horses over the fences — I hoped he wasn't going to be as difficult as he appeared.

Moving off to spend time with my favourite boy, Elder, I watched as he and Honor dozed. In comparison to some of the others, they were very quiet and relaxed. Sitting quietly on a hay bale I picked up a book and made myself comfortable, reading out loud so the old grey stallion would become accustomed to my voice. Occasionally he turned to watch me, but mostly he rested; as he had been in the snow the winter before, he wasn't overly worried now about what was happening around him.

Argo's first river adventure, just five days out of the wild.

CHAPTER 5

Long hours

Top
Vicki touching the first of the wild horses.

Bottom
Vicki getting a close look at Hoff's head wound for the first time, as Amanda and Mum look on.

The next day Argo, Libby and the chestnut mare were taught to lead, and could be approached in an open area and touched on the head and neck. It was almost impossible to believe that they had been completely untouched the day before — now, with only a couple of hours of contact time, they were relaxed about standing beside us and being handled.

We still had lots of horses to work, so we released these three and brought Elder and Honor into the race for the second time. By the time we were finished with them an hour later, both were wearing halters and stood dozing while we brushed the dreadlocks from their manes and the dust from their coats. DOC and Tullock were also brought in and touched for the first time. The dapple grey stallion was the easiest of all the horses, while the little black lowered his head, trying to hide; but Vicki worked quietly with him and soon both were haltered. Hoping we could get Hoff in to work again we tried to draft him into the race, but we couldn't get him to go through the open gateway; with daylight running out, we decided to leave him for another day.

The following morning, Vicki and Amanda loaded some of the young showjumpers onto the truck for a training competition and I stayed home with Kirsty to make the most of the quiet yards. Before the others left, however, they came to the yards to help us get Honor and Elder into the race. The evening before the pair had been quite difficult, and when we'd entered the yard to feed them Honor had rushed at us and threatened to attack in an attempt to keep us away from Elder. With him almost crippled by lameness we understood that she was only trying to protect him, but it was important that we continue handling them, and it needed to be safe for us to do so.

Even with six of us trying to bring Elder and Honor through into the race it was difficult, and many times the protective mare faced us up; but finally she settled and stepped through the open gate, Elder limping closely behind. Once they were in the race they soon relaxed and Kirsty and I began untangling Elder's dreadlocks. It takes years for a horse's tail to reach full length, and because every strand of Elder's was entrapped in the dreads it didn't seem right to cut his entire tail off — so we were committed to untangling it. I was lucky that the others were at a show, because otherwise, with so many horses to work, I wouldn't have had the opportunity to spend so much time in the race with just one horse. We worked from the bitter chill of dawn right through to the midday heat, Elder standing patiently as we sat on the boardwalk, his tail threaded through the rails and spread across our laps.

Using hot water and litres of conditioner we slowly made progress, but it was a time-consuming task; by the third hour we were only halfway done. Kirsty grew bored and drifted a few metres back to interact with Honor; soon she was leading the mare up and down the race. Elder wasn't concerned, so she backed Honor out into a larger yard and began teaching her to lead, then stood quietly talking to her until she could touch her all over the head, neck and shoulders. I had been watching out of the corner of my eye and was amazed — the mare had gone from one of the most aggressive horses to the most advanced in just a couple of hours.

I had been working on Elder's dreads for five hours now and, deciding it was enough for the day, I led him forward into an open yard and stood holding out grass for him. To my surprise he pricked up his ears, stepped forward and picked the grass from my hands. Walking back to the fence, I picked another handful of grass and held it out for him — and again he stepped forward and pulled the grass from my outstretched fingers until it was all gone. Since he was so relaxed, I held out a hand and watched as he reached forward and bumped it with his muzzle. I was beyond elated. This old stallion seemed so gentle and wise, and I couldn't believe that after only four days he had approached me in a large area and initiated contact, or that he'd remained so relaxed about it.

Vicki and Amanda soon returned home, and were amazed by the progress we had made. True, we had spent seven hours with these two horses, but they weren't tired; instead they were relaxed and interested in everything that was happening around them — there had been no pressure put on them, merely good bonding time and an atmosphere of patience. Vicki *was* a little surprised that we'd spent the whole day with just two horses and asked why I wasn't working with Anzac — he was, after all, my sole challenge horse, and of the two it was more crucial that

the chestnut make progress. To be honest, I hadn't formed any sort of attachment to the little guy — he was smaller, plainer and more aggressive than several of the others. Shaking her head, Vicki said that I hadn't given him a chance, and turning to Amanda she suggested that we both get our challenge horses in. By this stage Vicki had haltered both her stallions and all three mares, and we were lagging well behind.

Anzac and Nikau were brought in first, and Vicki watched while we got the horses used to our hands on them, then secured the halter buckles on their heads. Both horses were more worried about being haltered than the others, and it didn't help that they were yarded together and were bringing out the worst in each other. Nikau was quite snappy with his teeth and Anzac often tried to rear to avoid being touched. Rather than reprimanding them, however, we ignored their antics and they soon settled down.

Biting, kicking and showing aggression is a natural part of the lives of wild horses. When they are foals their mother will use her hooves and teeth to keep them in line, and as they get older they fight each other to establish a hierarchy — especially the stallions, as they have to win herds of their own and then battle to keep them. Disciplining horses for this instinctive behaviour only gives them reasons to fear us, making them more inclined to try to hurt us. When we ignore the behaviour and instead make their experiences positive, they quickly learn that there is no reason to feel threatened. Of course if the horse is trying to hurt us for neither fear- nor pain-related reasons, that's a completely different story and they are told off for their bad behaviour; we have found this is rarely the case with wild horses in the initial handling.

The swivel of an ear, the tensing of muscles or the stamp of a hoof are all ways in which horses communicate with us, and as we worked with Anzac and Nikau we kept a close eye on their body language. As soon as they appeared worried, we slowed what we were doing or changed the way we did it. It was important to instil confidence in these horses rather than cultivate fear, so we allowed them to dictate what they were ready for. Nikau and Anzac soon relaxed under our gentle hands, and once they were haltered we let them back into their yard.

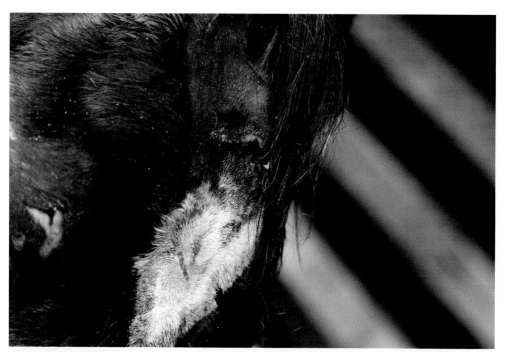

TOP
Hoff's head wound starting to heal over.

BOTTOM
Promise, Argo and Honor being led outside of the stockyards
for the first time, just five days out of the wild.

Next it was crucial that we work with Hoff; we were worried about his weeping head wound and wanted to get antibiotics into it as soon as possible. Like the previous day, the stroppy stallion wasn't interested in leaving his yard, but after 10 minutes he stepped through into the smaller yard that led into the race, and we swung the gate shut. Panicked, he spun and charged at the gate and attempted to jump it, hitting the top rail before dropping back to the ground. Scrambling forward, I climbed the rails so he wouldn't attempt it again and he stood below me, angrily pawing the ground and snorting furiously. For almost 20 minutes we tried to get him into the race, but since none of us felt safe entering the yard with him it was a trying process. Eventually we stood on either side with a sheet of canvas stretched between our hands, moving slowly closer to Hoff, hoping that this would encourage him to turn and move through into the open gateway. To our absolute horror the stallion reared instead, launching at the fabric with bared teeth and tearing it from our hands, mauling it. His fight response was far stronger than his flight one and didn't seem to back down from anything; it was the worst behaviour in a horse, either wild or domestic, that we had ever witnessed. Finally, we managed to get him to back through into the gateway and we swung the gate shut in front of him. Grasping the opportunity, we put some antibiotics in his head wound and haltered him before releasing him back into his larger pen. We narrowly missed being bitten on numerous occasions but knew that we might not get a second chance.

Bad weather was due any day now, and since it was the middle of winter we were trying to get the horses home as soon as possible. Vicki decided that Honor and Argo were ready to go home, so she loaded them on the truck through the cattle ramp and drove them to our property — both unloaded easily and were taken for a walk through the river before being put in the large covered yards for the night. Both horses were responsive to the leads and curious about their first adventure — even though it was their first time out in an open space since they had been mustered, they never tried to break free and calmly followed behind us.

Back at the stockyards Amanda and I were feeding and watering the horses for the night, and just as we were leaving there was a huge commotion. Spinning around, we watched as Tullock engaged one of the other stallions in full battle, rearing and striking out. Rushing forward to separate them, we watched in horror as he threw the smaller horse past his balancing point. The smaller horse toppled over backwards, crashing into the fence and splintering the rails as he fell to the ground. Opening the gate, we threw ourselves between the two stallions, trying to keep them separated; they prowled on either side on the fence, filled with adrenaline.

By the time we had the fence repaired it was well after dark, and we headed home exhausted. It had only been four days since the horses had arrived but already the long hours were taking their toll. However, regardless of how much time it took, the endless mud and the possibility of injury, it was worth it. Every time we made progress with the horses we were filled anew with a sense of purpose, and it was rewarding to watch them transition into future partners and willing friends — although Hoff seemed to disagree, finding fault with everything. But we were confident that even Hoff would have a change of heart, and hoped that he would soon realise we weren't there to hurt him. Anyone can force a horse to do something, and I'm sure that many trainers would boast that they can get faster results than us — but speed is not our focus and never will be. It takes skill, time and thoughtfulness to get a wild horse that is genuinely relaxed and happy about the process of domestication, and we were willing to take as much time as the horses needed.

CHAPTER 6

The calm before the storm

Only 10 days after he was mustered,
Anzac went to the beach for the first time.

The next morning Elder and Libby were trucked home, and that afternoon the chestnut mare, whom we had named Promise, was also ready. At the home yards we caught all of the Kaimanawas already there and led them down to the river for a change of scenery. They were curious, sensible and bold, and because we were short of a handler we left Honor loose and she followed closely behind. In hindsight they were all barely halter-broken and with three mares and two stallions it could so easily have gone wrong, but at the time we were enjoying the chance to show them something positive about domestication. They certainly enjoyed their walk across the arena, wandering in the water and then weaving through the trees on the opposite shore.

We led the horses into the deep water and took them for a swim, and even Honor followed. She quickly lost interest, though, and headed back to shore. One of the stallions was distracted by the mare and pulled away, trotting out of the water to follow her. With two horses loose we were careful to keep hold of the others while one of the girls who works for us ran through the trees in search of the wayward stallion. Soon she had him caught, and we laughed as she gently chastised the stallion for finding Elder's mare more interesting than a winter swim.

After we had led the horses back to the stables we handled a few of them; Elder stood dozing while I ran my hands gently over his face and braided his forelock. He was now yarded separately from Honor; there was no doubt that individually they were easier to handle, but even when reunited they were manageable. Both had behaved well during their river adventure.

Back at the neighbours' stockyards we still had five horses. Nikau and Anzac had improved dramatically and were now the most advanced of the ones down there. Anzac didn't yet understand the concept of leading, however, and the day before had dragged me all over the yards, my boots losing traction in the slippery mud. Amanda had also had problems with Nikau; he had started rushing at her with teeth bared if she got too close. A couple of times she'd been so scared that she had retreated and scaled the fences, and unfortunately the horse had quickly learnt that his intimidating behaviour was working in his favour. No amount of convincing from Vicki or me would make Amanda stand her ground; already a nervous mess after trying to work with Hoff, she wasn't willing to take the risk — she was convinced that these horses meant her harm.

Although the weather was so dismal that the yards were turning to mush, we spent an hour reinforcing Anzac and Nikau's lessons from the day before. Both had obviously done some serious thinking overnight, and had much better manners and were leading well. Soon they were loaded onto the truck and brought home, leaving just three problem horses at the stockyards.

Tullock, who'd initially been the quietest, was now grumpy around people and pinned his ears back if anyone approached; Amanda was too nervous to work him. Fear is a funny thing. After just a few days working with the Kaimanawas, Amanda had lost so much confidence that she dreaded going down to the yards. Since Tullock wasn't entered in the Stallion Challenges, she asked Vicki to do some work with him and Vicki quickly agreed. Deciding that he would benefit from being worked off the back of another horse, Vicki saddled up her trained palomino Spotlight and rode into the yard to work the dapple grey. Soon he was respecting both horse and handler, accepting Vicki's touch and following behind the trained horse as they circled the yard. Confident that he was now ready to be taken home, she loaded him onto the truck through the race.

DOC also benefited from being handled off Spotlight, and Vicki worked with the little black stallion for an hour until he could be touched on the head and was good to lead. Unlike the others DOC was shy and stressed; with his head-shaking and wind-sucking issues, Vicki was sure that something was wrong with him, and it was important to get him quiet enough to handle so that she could begin to diagnose the problem. Since he was more introverted and reactive than the others, she decided to lead him home over the farm rather than take him back on the truck. At first he dragged on the rope but soon gained confidence and kept up with the larger horse, trotting on the lead, alert and interested as they made their way towards home. Forty minutes later, as they turned down the driveway, he was relaxed and walked between two ridden horses, both riders resting a hand on the stallion's back.

Hoff was now the only Kaimanawa at the stockyards and we had taken a few showjumpers down to keep him company. He was a totally new playing field for us — his aggressive behaviour, while excusable because of the pain he must have been enduring, was something we hadn't encountered before. He was the first truly savage horse we had ever met, the type of untameable stallion you read about in books, and we were always very careful around him. We had no doubt that, if we got ourselves in a position to be hurt, he would get us on the ground with intent to kill, just like wild stallions that fight to the death.

The most unsettling thing about Hoff was the extremes in his personality; he would lure us in with an appearance of calm. Most of the time in the yards he was relaxed with his ears forward, and always stood watching us. It was only when we approached that he would throw himself at the fence and try to attack us through the rails. We had no trust in him and never entered his yard unless we had a well-thought-out plan — we didn't want to have to retreat, as this would only reinforce his bad behaviour. Unfortunately, it was crucial that he be handled so that we could get him out of the stockyards because the weather was worsening and the conditions in the yards were less than ideal.

Although the trainers were supposed to work exclusively with their challenge stallions, Amanda was long past the point of managing Hoff alone. At this point the most important factor was the horse's welfare. Amanda knew that she didn't have the experience or the bravery to deal with such a difficult horse and was willing to do whatever it took to ensure that he had the best chance of making progress. Again she asked for Vicki's help, and Vicki agreed.

While it was obvious that Amanda was out of her depth, Vicki wasn't sure that anyone else would be more successful. Knowing her options were limited, Vicki decided to try to enter the stallion's yard on Spotlight's back, hoping she'd be safer on the back of another horse. Although Hoff was quite aggressive, the experienced palomino quickly put him in his place and Vicki was able to herd him into the race and get a rope on his halter. From there she tried to teach the horse to lead, but Hoff alternated between dragging on the rope and rushing forward to attack.

For almost two hours Vicki worked with him, and made no real progress. Finally it got to the point where it was decided to bring him home anyway. A severe storm was due, and leaving him in the stockyards wasn't an option with the threat of rising floodwaters. After much thought we decided that trucking him home would be too dangerous, so everyone saddled horses to help get him home over the farm. Although it was a hair-raising ride, Vicki, on Spotlight, managed to keep hold of the stallion as he fought to get loose, and the other horses and riders kept him in line as much as possible. The ride took three times as long as it should have, and there were times when tempers flared as people realised just how dangerous the situation was. Even the other horses feared the black stallion, and no one wanted to get too close in case he hurt someone.

Everyone was almost home when Hoff threw himself at a fence, going straight under the wires. Although he was uninjured, suddenly they had a dilemma on their hands. Vicki was sitting on Spotlight on one side of the fence while on the other side the black stallion struggled to get free, pulling on the rope. Bracing himself, the palomino stood his ground while around them the other riders quickly dismounted and handed all the horses to one of the girls to free up extra hands. Loosening the rope, Vicki dismounted and quickly wrapped the rope around a post, managing to keep hold of the stallion while someone led Spotlight through a gate and brought him to her. Remounting, she took hold of the rope again and they continued on their way. Soon Hoff was safely contained in the home yards; although it had been a terrifying journey, at least he was safe and above flood level if the coming storm was as bad as we feared.

OVER THE NEXT FEW DAYS THE WEATHER continued to hold despite the promised storm, and with the exception of Hoff every horse was making progress. Some were so good, in fact, that we sometimes forgot they were wild horses. Just eight days after the muster, on the afternoon after Hoff had been brought home, Vicki took Honor out in the paddock and backed her. She was sweet and curious, and stood quietly while Vicki lay all over her bareback; she didn't even shift when Vicki swung a leg over and sat astride. For half an hour Vicki sat scratching the mare, and Honor

Top
Grazing Elder and Anzac in the paddock.

Bottom
Vicki backing Honor for the first time — she loved being scratched.

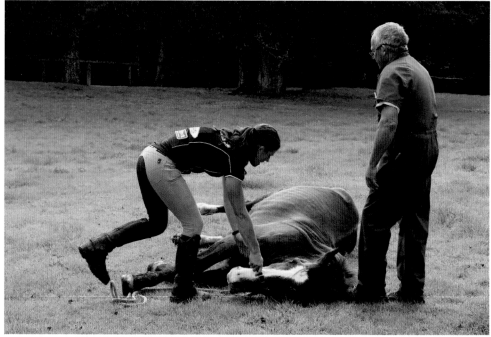

TOP
Vicki lying across Argo's back, eight days after the muster — the
first of the Stallion Challenges horses to be backed.

BOTTOM
Argo sedated and about to be gelded.

bent her neck around and tried to scratch Vicki's leg in return. They even went for a little walk before Vicki jumped off, worried — the mare was slightly lame in one leg. Vicki took her into the stables to wash down her legs. With the mud rinsed from her hooves, the damage to one hoof wall was obvious: a crack ran right up through the cornet band. It was one of the worse cases we had seen, and Vicki made a note to get the vet to see Honor when he was out to geld the first stallions the following day.

Deciding that Argo was also ready to be backed, Vicki caught her challenge horse and led him onto the arena. Working quietly, she jumped up and down beside him to get him used to the motion, and since he stood calmly she vaulted onto him and lay across his back. Nothing seemed to worry the large horse, and within a few minutes Vicki swung a leg over and slowly sat up, then asked him to walk and trot around the arena. He was relaxed and steady beneath her and, because she was riding him bareback with only a halter to guide him, Argo wasn't unsettled by the feel of a saddle or bridle and listened carefully and was very responsive — he already had a good bond with Vicki. Her goofy giant was proving to be very level-headed. It was hard to believe that a week before he had been running wild in the Kaimanawa Ranges.

Although Amanda and I were a long way from backing our own challenge horses, we were happy with our progress. Anzac was now eating out of my hand and Amanda felt safe leading Nikau, although she only touched him through the safety of a fence. She had lost so much confidence from working Hoff that she was even scared around her showjumpers, let alone the wild horses, and it was worrying to see how much she'd deteriorated in just over a week.

I knew what she was going through; I'd had three near-death experiences in the past few years. The first had been a near-miss with rattlesnakes in the Grand Canyon, the second time I'd fallen off a cliff snowboarding, and the third time I'd written my car off when I'd crashed into a bridge at night. Although plenty of time has passed since these incidents I still scream every time I see a snake (even if it's only on television), avoid snowboarding near cliffs in icy conditions, and am very cautious driving in the dark on wet roads. It's simply a matter of self-preservation and instinct to try to avoid similarly dangerous situations in the future.

Countless times now Hoff had charged at people, and both Vicki and Amanda had seen their lives flash before their eyes during his attacks. Although he hadn't managed to injure anyone yet, Amanda feared being hurt by him and was often reduced to tears imagining worst-case scenarios. Many times in that first week she begged to be allowed to quit, but each time we encouraged her to keep trying and, although she avoided Hoff as much as possible, she slowly gained the trust of Nikau. Amanda was also working with Tullock again, and they were making good progress since he had returned from the stockyards.

IT WAS NOW NINE DAYS SINCE THE MUSTER and our vet was due to geld the first lot of stallions — far sooner than we would usually do it, but he was going overseas and we preferred to use a vet we knew was experienced and patient with the wild ones. Starting with the easiest, Argo was led out to the paddock and our vet quietly approached. Although not used to strangers, Argo stood quietly while he was injected and soon dropped to the ground, fast asleep, and the vet got to work. DOC and Nikau, who were slightly more wary, were given an oral sedative first and we waited an hour for it to have its full effect before the vet approached. This worked well, and soon we had three geldings in the process of waking up, their days as stallions behind them.

With daylight running out there was time for just one more, and although he was the least handled it was agreed that Hoff should be attempted so that we could also treat his head wound while he was on the ground. Saddling Spotlight up, Vicki rode into Hoff's yard and quietly worked with him, managing to avoid being bitten as she got the sedative under his tongue. An hour later, when he was at his sleepiest, she rode back into the yard and used Spotlight to manoeuvre him against the rail so that the vet could sedate him fully from behind the safety of the fence. Before long he staggered and dropped to the ground. He too was soon gelded, his feet trimmed, the infected hole in his skull cleaned out and treated, and while he was under we took a quick peek at his front teeth to determine his age — he was the oldest of the horses we had gelded that day, and looked to be about 13 years old.

Next we brought Honor into the wash-down bay. She stood while her hoof was lifted, trimmed and shod — the damage was extensive and needed urgent veterinary care. Honor was sedated for the surgery, and stood quietly while holes were drilled into the hoof wall and then stitched with wire so that the two sides of the hoof could be stabilised, then reinforced and protected with special glue. The mare had obviously been suffering for a long time in the wild. The damage would have continued to worsen without human intervention; she was lucky to have been mustered.

The following day we loaded Honor onto the truck for her first beach adventure; the salt water would be good for her hoof and it would be a nice change of scenery for her. Anzac and Promise also joined her and we spent time teaching them to load up the ramp of the truck. It didn't surprise us when Honor, who was the most unwild wild horse we had ever encountered (when not in cahoots with Elder, that is!), walked straight onto the truck. Even Anzac was loaded within minutes — the young stallion was quite food-orientated and willingly followed a handful of hay up the ramp. Promise took a little more convincing but bravely followed the others, stepping one foot at a time up the ramp and standing tensely while the divider was closed. Next we loaded the showjumpers so that the Kaimanawas would have the reassurance of domesticated horses on their adventure, and finally we were on the road.

All three Kaimanawas were confident at the beach. We led Anzac and Promise behind the showjumpers, while Honor strolled along beside us at a sedate walk, with Vicki sitting on her — now that her hoof was stabilised she was sound; the vet had assured us that she could continue with light work. After splashing in the waves we led the horses back to shore and they rolled in the dry sand as evening set in, completely relaxed and loving life. Slowly, we made our way back to the truck. Honor and Promise walked straight onto it, but Anzac must have decided that he didn't want to leave, because he refused to load and reared and dragged on the rope for over 40 minutes before he gave up and slowly walked up the ramp as if he didn't have a care in the world.

TOP AND BOTTOM
Stitching Honor's hoof with
wire to stabilise the hoof wall.

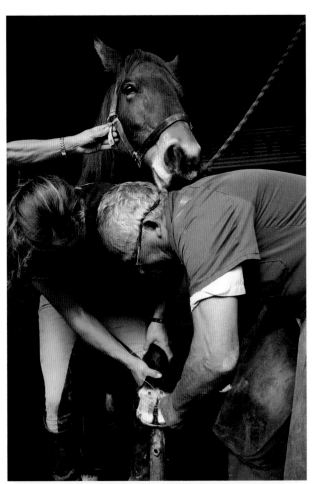

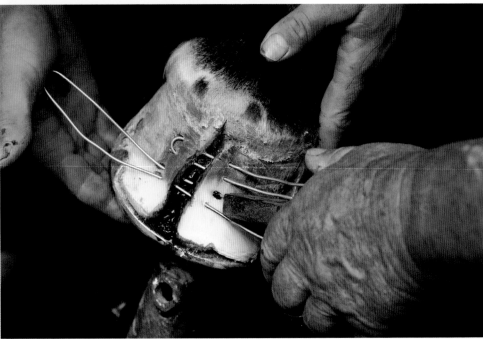

Although the horses still had their moments, overall there was a quiet sense of awe among us; we were amazed at how quickly and happily these horses were adjusting to domestication. They were far more advanced than our horses from the previous muster had been, having reached this stage within half the time. The experience we had gained from the Kaimanawas over the past two years was helping to make the transition much more seamless.

CHAPTER 7

One step forward, two steps back

In the days following the flood, Elder became so aggressive we tried to work him off horseback, but he wouldn't tolerate Spotlight being close.

Elder enjoying some time
in the paddock during
a break in the rain.

Elder had been making such huge progress that we decided to reunite him with Honor. They had seen each other in passing over the past week, but hadn't been yarded together since they'd been brought home from the stockyards. Leading him over, I released him into the round pen beside Honor's yard and let him loose. He made his way towards her, neighing — I winced as he limped over to the rails — and talked to her through the fence, standing as close to her as possible. Watching how they interacted intrigued us — they seemed to share a very strong bond.

Later that evening I returned to catch Elder. Approaching slowly, I walked towards him and as soon as he saw me he pricked up his ears and started coming towards me. After a couple of strides I paused, however, and my smile faded. His muscles were coiled and, as he drew closer, he leapt towards me with bared teeth and ears pinned back. This wasn't a welcome; it was a warning! Growling at him, I held my ground until he retreated and then I left the yard, running back to the stables to get reinforcements.

It was the first time that Elder had ever threatened me, and with one of the girls at my side I returned to attempt to catch him a second time. Over the next few minutes he rushed at us three times, but after he'd learnt he couldn't intimidate us he backed down and I was able to walk up and catch him. Once he was caught he settled down a little and followed us back to the stables. Reuniting the two horses had been a mistake, and it was only the beginning of our problems.

The next day Elder was difficult and unpredictable. He no longer wanted to be touched, and when I approached he would snap his teeth and toss his head away. Persevering, I worked with him and finally he stood while I touched his head; wanting to finish on a good note, I then put him away. He wasn't the same horse I'd handled so easily just 24 hours before. His behaviour was threatening and I knew he was fully capable of hurting me if I made a wrong move.

To make matters worse, we were now experiencing some of the worst weather in years. It had been raining for days and the entire property was muddy and waterlogged. All the Kaimanawas were off the paddocks

TOP
Libby, wearing a cover for the first time, during the worst of the storm.

BOTTOM
Amanda and Nikau walking through the last of the floodwater the morning after the storm passed.

and in yards, and working with them was a miserable but unavoidable experience. Two horses in the region had already died from exposure to the weather, and with a severe weather warning in place for the rest of the week we decided to get as many of the Kaimanawas as possible into rugs.

Argo stood quietly while the rug was tossed over his back, not minding when the back straps were done up even though Vicki had not touched him that far back before. Honor, Libby, Promise, Anzac, Tullock, Nikau and DOC were a little unsure, so we rubbed them with towels before approaching them with rugs. The person holding the horses had a difficult job managing them as they leapt forward at the unfamiliar feel of the covers. Doing up the straps was an even more hazardous experience, during which Vicki, Amanda and I all avoided well-aimed kicks from a few horses that had had little handling.

Since Elder and Hoff couldn't be touched at all, both were led into the stables to stay dry; there was no way we could have put rugs on them. With the storm at full fury and no sign of it lessening in intensity, it was crucial that Elder and Hoff have the added protection; the trees alone weren't enough to shelter them, and after days of constant rain the horses' skin was starting to rot and slough off.

That night we experienced gale-force winds and torrential rain. The following morning I was jolted from sleep by Vicki as she pulled open my curtains. Sitting upright with a start I looked out the window — where there should have been paddocks and fences, all I could see was water. I hurriedly dressed and followed Vicki outside. Amanda was already moving horses; pointing towards Anzac's yard, she threw me a rope. I stumbled, still half asleep, to where he stood in the water; as soon as I stepped into the cold floodwaters I was wide awake. Wading through the muddy water I caught Anzac; relieved, he eagerly followed me through the gate, out of his yard and up onto higher ground.

The showjumpers were safe in the hill paddocks, with covers on and plenty of trees for added shelter, but even they were losing hair and skin on their polls, ears and above their eyes — anywhere exposed to the weather. Vicki couldn't wait for her new stable complex, which had just started construction, to be finished so that more horses could remain under cover in bad weather.

For the next hour we moved Kaimanawas into the higher yards; but if the rain didn't stop soon, we weren't sure whether even these would remain above the flood level. Unfortunately we couldn't move them up onto the hill, as none of them could yet be trusted in the paddocks. We were lucky we had got Hoff home three days earlier because he couldn't have stayed in the neighbours' stockyards, knee-deep in mud with no shelter from the relentless rain.

That night we prepared for the worst. The water had continued to rise and, although every Kaimanawa was on dry ground, we were worried about how much worse it would get — this was the worst flood we had had since the 150-year flood seven years earlier. The arena was already under water — to get to the mares that were yarded on the far side of the property, we had to wade through thigh-deep water holding hay above our heads. By dusk the Kaimanawas were settled and we headed inside to dry off.

It was a relief to wake up to sunshine and blue skies; the storm had finally passed. Over the course of that day all of the water disappeared, almost as though the flood had never happened. Since the horses were all unaccustomed to being rugged, we caught the Kaimanawas and began uncovering them. For some it was a more complicated task than covering them had been — in some cases it took an hour to get a rug off.

Many of the horses were grumpy after days of rain, wind and confinement, so we took them for walks on the arena so they could stretch their legs. Elder was the most difficult he had ever been — if anyone approached too close, he would lunge at them. He was also at his lamest and was stiff when he moved; after days in the stables his legs were swollen. As he limped slowly around the arena I was careful to maintain a respectful distance — I no longer trusted him and knew that, like Hoff, every time I worked with him there was an element of risk.

Although the other Kaimanawas were fairly easy in comparison, we were still careful to only let experienced people handle them. The occasional accident was unavoidable, however. That night, during evening feeds, one of our girls entered Nikau's yard to put hay in his trough, and as she turned to leave he swung his head around and sank his teeth into her upper arm. The bite grazed her skin, leaving an indent of teeth marks on both sides of the muscle, and his canine teeth caused a puncture wound. Badly shaken, she came inside; within minutes, the bruising was severe and the swelling took months to go down.

It was now two weeks since the muster, and our early optimism and confidence were rapidly deteriorating. While some of the horses were easier than we had ever experienced, there was no doubt that others were our biggest challenges yet. Even Vicki, who normally gets such good results with her horses, was struggling with DOC. He was still wind-sucking and head-flicking constantly, and the only time he'd been at ease was when he'd been on serious pain-killers in the days following his gelding. Vicki had no doubt that his symptoms were pain-related but he wasn't at a point where he could be handled enough to work out what was wrong with him.

Luckily, with so many horses at different levels, there was always something positive happening and every day saw something rewarding. Although Elder continued to worsen, Anzac was progressing well and I was having lots of fun teaching him new things. Amanda was also feeling much more confident around Nikau and they were forming a good bond; he was the easiest of the Kaimanawas to catch now and was the first to have his halter taken off. This was a significant milestone — we only remove halters when we are confident that a horse can be approached in an open area and will stand relaxed enough to be caught. Likewise, Tullock was coming along nicely. It was good for Amanda to start making progress with them; it gave her some confidence back. Gradually, she began working with Hoff again.

Apart from DOC, Vicki's horses were miles ahead of ours. Each day, she worked her stallions, then the girls helped her work the mares. Honor was our firm favourite; she genuinely loved attention and being ridden. Because of her hoof surgery, her rides generally consisted of five minutes of walking and then Vicki would sit on her in the middle of the arena, scratching her for 40 minutes while she talked the girls through the process of handling, then backing, Promise and Libby. It was an awesome

Top
Vicki riding Argo at the beach with the showjumpers for the
first time, with Anzac and Nikau being led.

Bottom
Argo's second ride and first canter was a déjà vu moment — he reminded
us so much of Major, our late stallion from the 2012 muster.

— 92 —

experience for Paula, Kirsty and Alexa to work through the entire process of taming wild horses, and although we assisted in the background they did most of the work with the mares.

Argo was also special, and each time Vicki worked with him everyone was impressed by his attitude to life. Just 18 days after the muster, Vicki took Argo to the beach for the first time and had her second ride on him. Again she took him out bareback in a halter alongside the showjumpers, while Amanda and I led Anzac and Nikau. Many times we shook our heads in wonder at how special this young horse was; it was a magical evening. As the sun set, Vicki cantered him down the beach and we had a moment of déjà vu — it was uncannily like the time Vicki had first cantered her old stallion, Major, down the beach two years earlier.

Happy with Argo's progress, Vicki jumped off and let him roll in the sand. She then offered to hold Anzac so I could back him for the first time. I was confident that he was ready, and although we were on the beach, with no fences in sight, I was sure he would be settled during the process. Gradually I accustomed him to my weight, lying over him, and for the first few times letting Vicki take most of my weight so that the young horse wouldn't be unsettled. A couple of times I moved too abruptly and he flicked an ear back in worry, but soon I was sitting astride him. He stood quietly as I patted his neck and told him what a good boy he was. For me it was hard to comprehend that I had backed my wild stallion in less than three weeks and it gave me great confidence. I was doing far better than I'd expected.

CHAPTER 8

Quality of life

DOC spent most of his time with his poll hyperflexed and sucking in air to cope with the pain he was suffering.

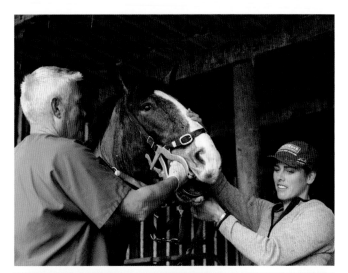

The following day our equine dentist, Warwick, was due to check the showjumpers. We were also hoping that a few of the Kaimanawas would tolerate a stranger so that they could have their teeth done and also be aged from their teeth. Argo was the first to be checked; as Vicki had thought, he was only a baby — he would officially be three years old in August so was only just old enough to compete in the Kaimanawa Stallion Challenges.

Although we had only planned to check his age, Argo was so relaxed that Warwick began working on his teeth. Within minutes it was obvious he had some serious dental issues, with Warwick removing handfuls of bloody grass from his lower jaw. One of his teeth was growing out of alignment, causing food to build up and rot in his jaw socket. There was no doubt that the diseased area would have affected his ability to survive in the wild. He would have been lucky to have lived to eight or nine years of age.

Because of Argo's severe issues, and in light of how easy he had been, we caught a few of the other Kaimanawas and led them over to be checked. Promise was four years old, Libby and Anzac five, Honor six and Nikau nine; these five were all text-book wild cases with sharp edges and hooks as well as some caps and wolf teeth that had to be removed, but in general they had good teeth with no major issues. Tullock also had good teeth and, as we'd expected due to his colouring, he was younger than the vet at the muster had thought. At only six years old, it was hard to conceive that without our intervention he would have gone to slaughter because he'd been deemed too old to re-home.

The next horse we checked was DOC. Vicki was very interested to see whether there was anything that would explain his symptoms. Every day our concern for DOC had increased, and as an experiment we had put him back on pain-killers to see if that would help. Like the days immediately following his gelding, DOC dramatically improved and was more relaxed and easier to handle.

After sedating DOC to ensure he was manageable, Warwick checked his teeth and we were disappointed to learn that he was about 15, older than we'd hoped. He also had a number of issues, including two fractured teeth, and there was a chance that the pulp chambers had become exposed, which is excruciating for horses. Concerned that this was causing DOC's behavioural issues, Warwick asked us to take DOC to a clinic in Auckland where he could investigate further using more advanced facilities.

With Warwick worried about DOC's fractured teeth, I was instantly concerned about Elder and we brought him in for Warwick to look at. Often when he'd tried to bite me I had caught a glimpse of missing front teeth. Although Warwick couldn't get close enough to Elder to check his teeth, we were at least able to get some photos by parting his lips with a brush connected to a broom handle. At least six of his front teeth were broken off; even more concerning were the horizontal fissure lines which were evident in all of the teeth. It looked as though the teeth were breaking off along these lines, and it was impossible to know whether this was from trauma, such as a kick, or whether he had brittle teeth from a dietary imbalance in the Ranges. Although ageing from photos is never accurate, the images showed the grooves in his teeth and the wear, and Warwick was able to give us a rough idea of his age. In keeping with the stories we had heard from the army and the musterers, the condition of Elder's teeth showed that he was the oldest of all the horses in the latest muster, although a more accurate ageing would have to be done once he could be handled.

OVER THE NEXT WEEK WE DID SOME light handling with DOC in preparation for the vet trip, and also taught him to load. To make sure he would be okay for the three-hour truck drive to Auckland, we decided to take him to the beach for his first trip to give him a positive experience. Tullock, Libby, Honor, Promise and Anzac joined him, along with Revelation from the 2012 muster. The three wild mares were ridden and were all quite relaxed until Honor stood on a flounder, leaping 3 metres in the air and sending Kirsty flying. Rather than stay with the other horses or head for shore, Honor powered through the estuary, heading out into deeper and deeper water until only her head was visible. Realising that she had no intention of returning, I jumped on Revelation and trotted through the water, eventually catching Honor and leading her back to the other horses.

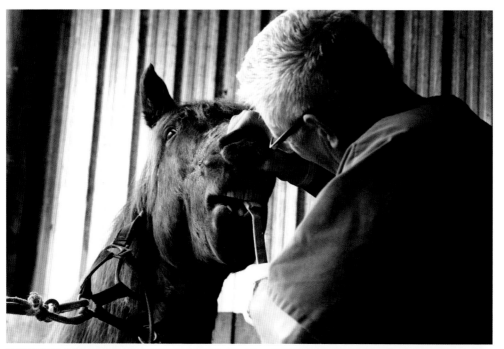

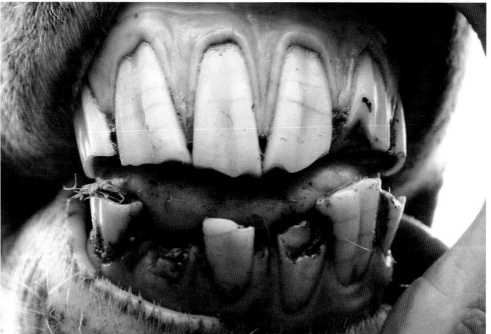

Top
Warwick working on DOC's teeth. One of the fractures can be seen on his front tooth.

Bottom
The number of broken teeth in Elder's mouth was a cause for concern,
but he wasn't handled enough for the dentist to work on him safely.

We had planned to back Tullock in the water for the first time, but a storm arrived out of nowhere and soon we were drenched and shivering. Returning to the truck, we loaded the horses and headed for home. It had been a chaotic morning but most of the horses had enjoyed it, although DOC still looked pained and withdrawn. We'd kept him on pain-killers for a few days after his teeth had been looked at, but with his vet appointment approaching we had taken him off everything so they could see him at his worst, without any of his symptoms masked. DOC was clearly suffering and we needed to find a way to help him as soon as possible, for both his comfort and our peace of mind.

Back at home, Vicki caught Argo in the paddock; like Nikau, he was now so friendly that he didn't need a halter on to be caught, although he was quite head-shy where his tooth abscess had been. Vicki brushed him all over, and Argo stood while she put a saddle on him for the first time. The rest of us prepared the showjumpers so that he would have company for his first farm ride. Taking her time, Vicki leant her weight over him. He didn't appear concerned by the unfamiliar feel of a girth and stood steadily. Swinging a leg over, Vicki mounted properly and soon we were on our way. Argo confidently took the lead and trotted happily along the track, and when we reached the hill he cantered alongside the more experienced horses. It was only his third ride, and the first under saddle, but he behaved like he'd been doing it for years.

While many trainers use old saddles for breaking in horses, for fear the saddles will be damaged, we do the opposite. Our Stübben saddles might be expensive, but they fit the horses superbly and we are firm believers that prevention is better than cure. So many young horses are poorly introduced to ridden life and develop behavioural issues that are avoidable. By ensuring that the horses aren't sore in their bodies, the saddles fit correctly and their teeth are done before introducing them to a bridle, there is no pain associated with being ridden; rarely do our young or wild horses buck under saddle.

We also want the horses to see ridden work as an adventure, so we spend minimal time in enclosed spaces or on the arena and try not to make things too repetitive. Instead, we get them out to the beach and on the farm — the wild horses especially look forward to being out in wide-open spaces.

With Vicki making such good progress, Amanda decided that Nikau and Tullock were ready to be backed. Since the weather was bad, she led them into the covered yards and began jumping up and down beside their shoulders to get them used to her moving like that close by. Once they were standing quietly, she asked Vicki to come in and help. She gave her a leg up onto Tullock; he was completely unfazed by the process and within a few minutes Amanda was lying on his back.

Next Amanda worked with Nikau. Although easier in general, he was a little more flighty and didn't like the weight of a person. Eventually he, too, settled and she was able to sit astride him as well.

Then it was Anzac's turn. I took him out to the arena to work. Since the others were busy, I asked our 10-year-old neighbour, Jazz, to come and watch; I'd sat on Anzac twice now and, although I didn't need help, we never worked the wild horses without someone else around just in case something went wrong. Anzac was quiet and relaxed, and I was soon leading him over a see-saw, and even got him standing with all four hooves on a small wooden box. Jazz couldn't believe how well-behaved he was and asked if she could have a turn; apart from me he'd never been handled by others, and I handed her the rope somewhat tentatively. Going through the motions, he performed all his tricks; Jazz was grinning from ear to ear as she led him back to the paddock. Before I had a chance to stop her, she unbuckled the halter and set him loose. In despair, I watched Anzac trot off; he still wasn't easy to catch and I hadn't planned on taking off his halter yet — and certainly not in such a large paddock.

To my surprise, he walked straight up to me when I returned to catch him that evening — I had thought I'd have to round him into a yard, but he stood for me while I looped a rope around his neck and was easy to halter. It was a great feeling.

FINALLY DOC's APPOINTMENT WITH THE VET ARRIVED; it had been exactly four weeks since the muster. Amanda had sold one of her showjumpers into Australia and he also had a vet check booked in

Auckland, so she and Mum loaded both horses on the truck and headed south. With plenty of other horses at home to work, Vicki and I stayed behind.

Once unloaded, DOC was very worried and almost impossible to hold. As the pain-killers had been withheld to allow the vets to see his true symptoms, there was nothing to numb the pain and he was aggressive and unpredictable. Even after the edge of his nerves was taken off with an oral sedative he was still too difficult for the vet or dentist to get near, and eventually he had to be blindfolded in a crush so that a second sedative could be injected. It was traumatic for both horse and handlers.

DOC was soon sleepy enough for the clinical examination to begin. The results were not promising. The pulp chambers were exposed on both of the fractured teeth, causing severe toothache, and several other teeth had signs of early fractures. Together with his other symptoms the prognosis wasn't good, and the vet advised that euthanasia was the best option to ease the pain and suffering that DOC was experiencing. It wasn't the news we had wanted to hear. Warwick offered a glimmer of hope: it was possible that invasive surgery and root-canal treatment on all 12 of DOC's front teeth could alleviate his distress, but there was no guarantee of long-term success and it was unlikely that he would ever break the habit of wind-sucking and head-tossing, which he'd developed to help manage the pain. Even if we decided to go ahead with surgery, it couldn't be done for several months because the horse needed to be standing during the procedure; even sedated, DOC was too wild to allow work on his teeth. It would be a terribly long waiting time for a horse that was living in constant agony, and although pain-killers would help it wasn't healthy for him to be living on them for weeks or months on end.

With so much to consider, Mum and Amanda had a quiet drive home and over the next couple of days we talked through our options. It was a hard decision to make, but after much discussion Vicki decided that it was in the horse's best interests to put DOC to sleep. She couldn't handle seeing him hurting so badly, and knowing that it would be a long road to get him ready for surgery she didn't think it was fair to subject him to ongoing pain, including later as the root canals failed over time. Traumatic though it was, we were glad that he'd been assigned to us and that we'd been able to understand the cause of his issues — many others might well have assumed he was just difficult to handle rather than searching for a solution to his symptoms.

Right from the start Nikau
had a cheeky personality and
suited Amanda well.

CHAPTER 9

The accidental bite

The decision to put DOC down was very difficult. During his five weeks in domestication he had made good progress and had come to trust us — when he was on pain-killers he was very sweet and content with life.

Bottom
Anzac trotting for the first time.

With Argo now Vicki's only horse suitable for the Stallion Challenges, she began investing some high-quality time in his training. Nothing seemed impossible for this gentle giant, and since she couldn't jump him, due to his young age, she began experimenting with new things he could do as part of his performance in the challenges. Deciding that he would be well suited to harness work she began teaching him how to pull a cart. Her first step was to teach him to respond on the long rein — within minutes, he was trotting around the arena while Vicki ran behind him. It was uncanny, really, how quickly Argo learnt new things. He was so in tune with Vicki that she only had to come up with an idea, decide to give it a go and Argo would quickly adapt, willing to try everything asked of him.

When Vicki came back to the stables after working Argo she was boasting about all the things he could do, just one month out of the wild; she was understandably very proud of how far he had come. Vicki decided that we needed some motivation with ours. I was always up for a challenge, so we set up a bet between us; she bet that I wouldn't have Anzac trotting under saddle and picking up all four feet within 72 hours, and I bet that she wouldn't have Argo pulling something within the same period. Amanda stayed quiet, and managed to avoid any challenges; instead, she offered to act as judge. Like all good bets, we were motivated by the incentives. I'd agreed to muck out the yards of 30 horses if Vicki was successful, and if I accomplished my tasks then Vicki had to shoe Anzac.

Deciding that there was no time like the present, I set to work rubbing my hands down Anzac's legs. He was very worried to start with, but soon settled and within 15 minutes I could pick up all four hooves — although he would quickly stamp them down and I wasn't yet able to hold each hoof up for the 20 seconds Vicki required.

Moving on to more pressing matters, I saddled him up and led him out to the arena. I was slightly apprehensive, but soon realised there was nothing to worry about: he wasn't at all concerned by the saddle and stood still as I mounted him. He was so unfazed by the whole process that within minutes I was able to turn around in the saddle and face backwards, stand up on him and slide over his rump. Confident that he was ready for his first walk, I asked him forward and then turned him in both directions before opening the gate and riding out into a larger area. His first ride under saddle had gone much better than expected, and I was sure he would be ready for his first trot the next day.

The next morning Vicki rode Argo on the arena, dragging ropes to get him used to having things behind him. Since he wasn't worried, she dismounted and attached a tyre to the end of the rope; Argo was soon dragging it while trotting quietly in circles — he couldn't have cared less about this random object bouncing along behind him. She had won her bet, and I resigned myself to some solid hours of mucking out.

Sure that Anzac was also ready to win our bet, I caught and saddled him and headed out to the arena. Urging him forward I asked him to trot, but instead he just walked faster. Time and time again I asked him to increase his pace, but each time he kept on walking. Trying to help, Vicki crowded in on Argo, riding close behind Anzac to push him forward. Annoyed, I told her to get out of my space — I didn't want Anzac to feel pressured into trotting, because that was when things were most likely to go wrong and I was already nervous enough. Again I squeezed with my legs, but again he failed to trot. Realising that I'd have to make my instructions clearer and apply more pressure with my legs I prepared to ask again, but before I had a chance I felt Anzac raise his head and eagerly step forward with a bounce in his step.

He was focusing on Kirsty pushing a wheelbarrow of hay in the distance! Knowing how much he loved his food, I gently nudged him with my heels again and this time he began trotting smoothly, his ears forward and all his attention on the hay in front of him. When he reached the wheelbarrow I asked him to slow, and he came back to a walk and then a halt before reaching forward and eating a mouthful of hay from the wheelbarrow, standing calmly while he munched.

I had often used hay to reward Anzac for learning new things, but I'd never thought to use it to entice him to trot. Stoked about my ingenuous discovery, I asked Kirsty to run around the arena pushing the wheelbarrow; again, Anzac trotted eagerly behind. Together we lapped the arena, until we had well and truly covered 100 metres. I had met the terms of the bet, with me exerting very little effort while poor Kirsty had got much more of a workout than she'd planned. It was unorthodox but it had certainly worked, and Anzac was loving the new learning experience — for him, trotting had just become a grand adventure with plenty of perks. For Vicki and me, however, the hard work was still to be done. I headed off to muck out her yards while she took Anzac back to the stables to shoe him.

THE NEXT DAY, THE FOURTH OF JULY, turned out to be a bad day in Wilson history. Things went from bad to worse. At dawn we said a heartbreaking farewell to DOC. Even though his fate wasn't what we had hoped for, we were glad that he'd been mustered; he would have had a slow and painful death in the wild.

That evening, Amanda and I were working with Tullock. It was the first time that the grey stallion had been ridden astride, but after 30 minutes he was walking quietly on the arena with Amanda riding him. At one point he was so relaxed he lay down and rolled underneath her; a surprised Amanda had to jump out of the saddle, laughing.

Impressed with how he was going, Amanda patted him and took him in for the night. Since Vicki was out and we were short of help, it was almost dark before we started feeding hay out to the horses. When I got to the Kaimanawas' yards Amanda was trying to cover Tullock, but although he'd been covered a number of times he was still unsure about it and was moving restlessly. Amanda asked for help, so I put the hay trailer down in the corner of his yard and held the rope while she did up the back cover straps.

Worried, he kicked out. Amanda asked me to get a better hold of him, so I reached up to grab his halter. Behind us, one of the other Kaimanawa stallions was trying to steal hay from over the fence and Tullock snaked his head to chase the other horse away. I was caught in the wrong place at the wrong time — instead of getting the other horse, his teeth closed over my arm, pulling me off my feet. As if in slow motion I watched him recoil backwards, and out of the corner of my eye I saw Amanda scrambling out of his way.

I glanced down at my arm and froze. My long-sleeved polo was ripped, and the torn fabric was lodged deep in a bloody crevice in my arm, covering much of the damage that Tullock's razor-sharp teeth had

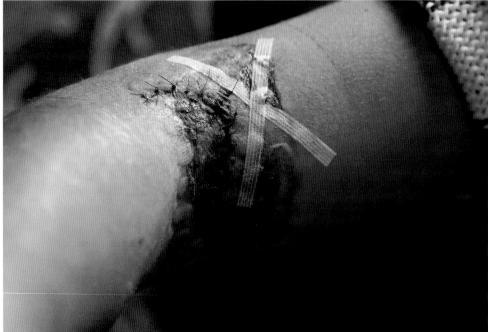

Top
Anzac eating hay out of the wheelbarrow after winning his bet.

Bottom
My bite looked much better after 13 stitches.

— 110 —

inflicted. What I could see was traumatising enough and pain was setting in fast; a burning agony that did justice to the gaping hole, about the size of my fist, on my inner elbow. Not wanting to know how bad it really was, I quickly averted my gaze.

My initial shock was followed by screaming. Amanda was gaping at me, white in the face. Abandoning the cover, she unclipped Tullock and helped me from his yard, and together we rushed to the car to drive to hospital. Blood was seeping down my side and through my clothes. By the time we reached the car, I was keening and others had come running — they'd heard the commotion from the other end of the property. When they saw the wound, their expressions confirmed my fears — it was indeed as bad as I'd thought. Amanda and Dad were trying to keep me calm and were telling me not to look down. Pressing a clean towel against my arm, Amanda jumped in the driver's seat and with shaking hands began the 40-minute drive to hospital — Vicki and Mum were already in town and promised to meet us there.

During the drive, I struggled not to black out. By the time we arrived at the hospital I was well and truly in shock; withdrawn and shivering, my teeth chattering uncontrollably. Mum and Vicki were already there and pried the towel off my arm to get a good look; the movement set the throbbing off again. Unsurprisingly, Vicki wasn't very sympathetic. Patting me on the shoulder, she joked about my low pain tolerance and told me that everything would be just fine. Completely miserable, I grouched that the horse had ruined my favourite polo shirt, and reassuringly Amanda promised to buy me another one.

Finally a doctor was ready to see me. I took plenty of pain-killers and made the most of the laughing-gas supply while I was stitched up. It wasn't until everything was pulled together that I had the courage to look at my arm again. With 13 stitches it wasn't looking anywhere near as bad, but I couldn't straighten my arm and it would be a long time before I'd be able to use it again — the last thing I needed when I had two wild stallions to tame and just 112 days until the first challenge.

CHAPTER 10

Injuries and setbacks

Anzac and the Kaimanawa mares about
to swim in the flooded river paddock.

I was up early the following morning, and to everyone's shock I started working with Anzac. It had taken a long time to get him to where he was now and I was worried that time off would send him backwards in his training. Although I couldn't ride, there was plenty we could still do on the ground. Trying to work with him with only one usable arm was challenging, though; I couldn't even get a halter on him. It was frustrating having to get others to help with even this most basic of tasks.

Two days later the school holidays started, and riders from all over the country arrived with their horses for our winter Showtym Camp. The Kaimanawas had been mustered from the wild only five weeks earlier and we were careful to keep them at the far end of the property, away from the chaos. Hoff was a serious concern to us and we were worried about having him on the property at all. Although he could now be led and handled to a certain extent, he was dangerous and aggressive and no one felt safe around him. Ever.

Hoff was a cunning animal. When anyone walked past his paddock, he would trot across to the fence and hang his head over the rail in greeting. It wasn't until some unsuspecting person reached out to pat him, or entered his paddock, that he would suddenly launch himself at them. When the kids arrived at camp they were all briefed about the dangers of approaching his paddock; we also lined his fence with *Warning*: *Do Not Enter* and *Don't Hassle Hoff* signs.

Unlike Hoff, we trusted Argo, Anzac and the mares around the kids, and the kids were all excited to watch the Kaimanawas being worked. Each horse was paired up with one of the camp riders to lead through obstacles, as part of team challenges, and even Anzac, who was still a stallion, was safe for them to handle.

Family friends had sponsored Anzac from the wild and the two oldest sisters from that family, seven-year-old Mouse and nine-year-old Livvy, were at camp and excited to spend some time with him. During his first few days out of the wild they had come to watch him being worked; back then he'd been one of the most difficult, and they were proud of how far he'd come in such a short time. Anzac's favourite child was Mouse, and he was always gentle around her. On the first day of camp she led him through the obstacle course on the arena and he was sweet and attentive. Confident that he would be quiet enough for her to ride, I asked her if she would like to hop on him. Turning to me, she asked how many times he'd been ridden; I told her that although he'd only been ridden under saddle twice, I had also ridden him bareback a few times and was sure he would be quiet for her.

She set to work helping me saddle Anzac, and he stood quietly for us despite not having been ridden in the three days since my bite. I wouldn't have put just any kid on him, though — there weren't many young riders as talented as Mouse. She'd been riding with us for a couple of years now, and she'd finished the season competing her pony in 1.05-metre showjumping classes and was experienced working with young ponies. She had an excellent feel with horses and I knew that if I told her to do something I could trust that she would listen.

Soon we headed out onto the arena, and Anzac was happy walking and trotting on the lead. Handing his rope to Livvy, I watched as the two young girls took him through the obstacle course and I couldn't help but smile — they were all having the time of their lives balancing on the swaying bridge and climbing onto the box with Mouse astride him.

That night it poured with rain and in the morning we woke to find the river paddocks under water. Making the most of all this water, the kids caught their ponies and swam them in the paddocks. They loved it, and when they were finished Vicki, Paula, Alexa and Kirsty kept everyone amused by trying to stay standing up on their horses while they swam. It wasn't long before all four girls could maintain their balance briefly while the horses were moving; I watched enviously from dry ground, wishing that my arm wasn't injured and I could join in the fun. To the camp kids' amusement, the girls never stayed upright for more than a few seconds before they fell head first into the water — it was very comical to watch. Vicki, who was on Argo, was hugely impressed that the young horse was coping so well with such bizarre antics.

Swimming in the paddocks was so much fun that Vicki and the girls decided Anzac and the mares needed to experience it too. Makaila, one of our friends, rode Anzac. Soon they were trotting through the

Top
Vicki losing her balance on Argo.

Bottom
Kirsty (in front) on Promise and Makaila on Anzac in the flooded paddock.

deep water and clearly loving it.

That night, inspired by the earlier attempts to stand up on horseback, we watched a movie about Lorenzo the Flying Frenchman who was famous for Roman riding. In between teaching the camp riders, Vicki decided this was something she needed to attempt, so, the next day, jumped on Argo bareback and strapped him beside one of her showjumpers. While Kirsty and Alexa rode the horses, Vicki stood behind them balancing with one foot on each horse's rump. Once she'd learnt how to balance, they unhooked the other horse and Vicki tried it with Argo on his own. Soon he was walking, trotting and cantering around the arena with Vicki standing precariously on his back — an amazing feat on a horse that had only been out of the wild for 41 days. Unfortunately this was not destined to be one of Vicki's real talents — more often than not she found herself falling off backwards.

Not long after, Vicki broke her wrist and collarbone when a client's horse reared over backwards on her. This naturally slowed her down, and she was bored out of her brain being unable to ride. It didn't stop her working, though, and every day she experimented, trying random new things with Argo; frequently we were left in hysterics. After a tree was felled, he stood to be strapped into harness and pulled the log from the river; another time Vicki carried a couch outside and spent an hour teaching him to sit on it, then took him into the house! Most of the things she never repeated; once she had accomplished something it became boring, and she moved on to conquer new challenges.

Amanda and I wavered between awe and frustration — there was no denying that Argo was spectacular, especially in comparison to our Kaimanawas, which were only at the most basic stages. Due to the bite on my arm it had been over a month since I'd been able to ride Anzac, and Amanda was still having difficulties with her horses. Of her three boys she had made the most progress with Nikau and had started riding him under saddle, although this hadn't been entirely successful: the first time Amanda asked Nikau to trot, she got bucked off three times in five minutes.

We don't often have a horse that bucks when it is first ridden, so Amanda ran her hands all over his body to see if he was sore anywhere.

Top
Amanda fell off three times while she was attempting to trot Nikau for the first time under saddle.

Bottom
Eventually Nikau settled and Amanda had her first trot and canter on him.

To her dismay, she discovered that he tried to bite and kick her when she touched around his wither area. Wearing a saddle had stirred up a nasty abscess that must have developed from wearing a cover over the past few weeks. This of course explained why Nikau had been so uncomfortable with a rider on him. Amanda had no other option but to turn him out into a paddock to rest — without a cover — and poultice the abscess daily.

With all of us sidelined to a certain degree — Vicki with her broken wrist, Nikau with his abscess and me still recovering from the bite — the next few weeks were quiet. Since all the mares were now cantering under saddle, we turned them out on the hills until they foaled. Making the most of the enforced down-time, we had the vet back out to geld the last three stallions: Anzac, Elder and Tullock.

The only Kaimanawas in consistent work were Hoff and Elder, after the latter had recovered from his gelding. Both were still a challenge, but since they had pain-related issues we were giving them the benefit of the doubt, hoping that they would adjust with time. Unlike Hoff, Elder had improved a little and I had regained some of my trust in him; as long as I didn't attempt to touch him he showed no aggression. After my mishap with Tullock, I wasn't prepared to risk another body part by pushing him; I knew that with enough time he would learn to trust me.

Although less advanced than the other horses, Elder was making good progress. Every day he walked up to eat grass out of my hand, and I had worked out a way of catching him so that he could live in a paddock. It was rather complicated catching a horse that refused to be touched! However, I was able to clip his lead onto a short rope hanging from his halter, although this could be a painstaking and time-consuming process — sometimes it took minutes and at other times it would take half an hour to secure the rope on him. Once caught, Elder was relaxed on the lead and would follow me anywhere. I could now lead him around the farm and, although still lame, he was moving much more easily and loved being led out while the girls rode the other horses. While the showjumpers cantered up the hills, I would lie resting in the grass with Elder standing beside me, eating, sometimes just centimetres from me.

Mouse and Anzac on the last day of our Showtym Camp.

TOP
Hoff trying to bite Vicki.

BOTTOM
Hoff trying to bite Amanda.

Deciding that the beach would be a grand adventure for Elder, I taught him to load in the truck. The first time, Elder refused to put so much as a hoof onto the ramp and alternated between rearing and darting to the side. After 40 minutes, he finally placed one hoof on the ramp and I rewarded him with a handful of grass and put him away for the night. The next day we started where we had left off, and within a few minutes he was loaded. Turning him around in the confines of the truck was daunting; I was worried that he would panic with a person so close to him. Jumping up onto the bench, I crawled out to give him as much room as possible to turn in — which he did calmly. Leading him off the ramp, we practised loading a couple more times before closing the divider and bringing the other horses over to join him.

From a purely logical perspective, taking a wild stallion I couldn't touch to the beach made no sense, but I wanted him to have an enjoyable experience in the hope that he would start making better progress. And from the moment Elder stepped off the truck and saw the ocean for the first time he was happy, wading in the cold water and rolling in the deep sand. Because everyone else was riding, we were often left behind, but even with the other horses out of sight Elder remained relaxed and content. It seemed ridiculous how much I could do with him and yet at the same time how little — at times it was hard to wrap my head around.

Although Elder and Hoff were essentially at the same stage in their handling, there was a significant difference. Elder could now be trusted completely in the paddock and on the lead, and only became difficult if I tried to touch him; but Hoff was always dangerous and unpredictable. Once Hoff had been caught Amanda could touch him on the head, but she had to keep a fence between them and always kept a firm hold on the noseband so that he couldn't bite her — and trust me, he always tried.

Amanda was desperately hanging on to the hope that Hoff's issues were simply pain-related. As well as the wound on his skull, which was now healing, she was sure that he had dental issues because we were finding balled-up wads of chewed hay on the ground every day and he wasn't gaining much-needed condition. Determined to at least diagnose him, she continued to work with him daily until he could be handled sufficiently. We had to give Amanda credit for persevering; many others wouldn't have bothered with such an ill-tempered horse. Finally, she was able to get the speculum on him, cranking his jaw open to check his back teeth. Like she'd suspected, Hoff's mouth smelt foul and we pulled out handfuls of rotting, half-chewed grass from the back of his jaw, indicating that there were serious issues. It was critical to get his teeth seen to as soon as possible.

The following week Warwick came up with the vet; the news was even worse than we'd anticipated. Three of Hoff's molars were diseased and unstable in his mouth, and had to be extracted under sedation. Once these were removed, it was obvious just how much the roots had decayed: only a few millimetres had been holding them in the jaw. Hoff must have had severe toothache for years. While it had been exhausting for Amanda to try to get Hoff handled enough to fix, it was a relief that she could now turn him out on the hills to recover in the company of other horses. A few months in the paddock would be the best thing for him, and she desperately hoped that when he returned to work he would be a different horse.

While Warwick and the vet were there, we were also able to do Elder's teeth under full sedation. To prepare him, I had been leading him into the crush each day and letting him doze while I groomed him. I was now able to touch him all over the forehead, neck and back, with him totally relaxed — although out of the crush he was still impossible to touch. Unlike DOC, Elder's broken teeth didn't seem to be cause for concern, which was a huge relief. Now that Warwick was able to get inside his mouth properly, he could get an accurate ageing from his teeth — instead of being 18, like we'd thought, Elder was between 12 and 16 years old. This was good news for us: he had many more years left in him, and I really hoped that with time he would accept first human contact and then a rider, because once he was sound I was confident that he would enjoy many adventures under saddle.

The hours I had already invested in Elder were huge and, like Amanda with Hoff, I would have loved nothing more than to turn him out to rest for a few months. Unfortunately, however, his lameness had gradually worsened again and was a real concern. He was now on pain-killers to help ease the discomfort, and even then he limped severely in the paddock and often stood rocking backwards and forwards to try to lessen the pain. After almost losing Momento, a grey mare from the 2012 muster, with severe foot abscesses, we knew how urgent it was to get Elder handled enough to treat and I increased the time I spent with him, hoping for a breakthrough.

Although it was a dangerous task, I finally got Elder to the point where I could touch him on the head and neck out in the open. He still greatly disliked being touched, and I came close to being bitten a number of times — I couldn't imagine being able to deal with his hooves. In despair, we called the vet — if we didn't do something drastic, Elder's feet could easily reach a critical point. We led Elder into the crush and sedated him, then led the drugged horse to the centre of the yard for a second injection. Even partially sedated he was too unpredictable for the vet to approach, but finally it was done — his knees buckled and he fell to the ground. Moving fast, we set to work; we had only 30 minutes before he would wake up. Vicki, Mum and the vet worked rapidly on his hooves — trimming them, dressing the bloody abscesses and then shoeing his front feet. Overnight the improvement was obvious: he was moving with far greater comfort, although he was a long way from being sound.

CHAPTER 11

The unwanted stallions

Vicki and Battlecry a
few days after he arrived
at our property.

TOP
Trooper in the muster yards.

BOTTOM
Battlecry crossing the river towards the yards during the muster. He had been number 9 in the Stallion Challenges draw, and was one of my favourites.

en weeks after the muster, we got a phone call from Kaimanawa Heritage Horses: one of the trainers in the Stallion Challenges had requested that his two horses be uplifted and re-homed urgently. Neither was gelded, both were still in yards, only one had been caught (with a lasso) and the trainer had tried to desensitise him with a sack, while the other had never been touched. The older bay, which the trainer thought was about 15 years old, was worried about life, and the younger chestnut appeared sweet but the trainer had never spent time with him.

There are very few trainers around the country with the resources, time and experience needed to take on older stallions from the wild, and with nowhere else for these horses to go we opened up our home and our hearts to them. There was no doubt that this was a huge burden. We had nine other wild horses at various stages of training and 18 of our showjumpers had just returned to work for the approaching competition season — but we were committed to doing right by the horses. It wasn't their fault that they had ended up in unsuitable hands.

Because Vicki had lost DOC, KHH offered her the older stallion as a second entry in the Stallion Challenges. At the muster, this stallion had been number 9 in the stallion draw — one of the two horses that had most caught my eye. If he could be ready in time, Vicki could compete him at the first event — in just 75 days; if not, he should be able to catch up by the finals in March. It was a win–win situation, and Vicki agreed to take him on and decided to call him Battlecry (Battle for short). She had high hopes that he would develop nicely under saddle and she was looking forward to the opportunity to train him to jump. Kirsty agreed to take on the younger stallion, and named him Trooper; he was to be the first wild stallion she would train unassisted.

Since neither horse had been handled, we had to load them through a stock ramp; both were obviously worried and stressed about life in captivity. Coming through the muster is a traumatising experience at the best of times, but positive interactions with humans can help the horses to adjust well in a very short amount of time. Instead, these two horses had suffered all the trauma from the muster and had then spent

TOP
Vicki about to halter Battle as he comes off the truck and through the stockyard race.

BOTTOM
Battle ate out of our hands for the first time on the morning after he arrived at our property.

the next two and a half months living in limbo, trapped in high-fenced yards, fearing humans and not realising that there was anything to look forward to. By this stage in the training process, our other Kaimanawas were in a much better place and frame of mind.

As the two stallions came off the truck at the neighbours' stockyards, Vicki and Kirsty began working with them immediately, getting them used to human contact in the crush and then releasing them into one of the larger yards. It was difficult for Vicki, who still had her wrist in a cast, but she was determined to handle Battle straight away — the sooner he learnt that humans could be nice, the sooner he would relax and begin to enjoy life.

The next day both horses ate out of our hands, and although shy and worried they were eager to have fresh grass — the first they had tasted since being mustered from their homeland. They had a natural curiosity and rapidly made progress; within days, both horses were leading well and Battle would stand still while being touched on the head and shoulders. Deciding that they were ready to come home, Vicki and Kirsty led them over the farm — it was the first time since the muster that the horses hadn't been surrounded by imposing fences, and both were happy and attentive, looking around curiously.

It is sometimes easy to get caught up in day-to-day life and lose sight of progress, but having these two new stallions on the property put everything into perspective. There were so many things that we had now come to take for granted with the other Kaimanawas, and having to start from scratch with Battle and Trooper only emphasised what we had accomplished with Argo, Anzac, Nikau, Tullock and the mares over the past two and a half months. The two new horses continued to progress quickly and, to our never-ending frustration, within a few days were already more advanced than either Elder or Hoff.

It was sad that Battlecry and Trooper's original trainer hadn't really given them the time they needed, because both horses genuinely wanted to please, and were sweet and willing; all they'd needed was a chance. What upset us the most was the trainer's clear disregard for the horses' ongoing care — he had made a commitment to taking horses from the

Vicki riding Battle for the first time, just nine days after he arrived at our property.

wild but, when he found out that it was more time-consuming than he'd thought, he quit and left it up to KHH to find a solution.

But his loss was our gain — and just nine days after we re-homed the pair, Vicki rode Battle for the first time. He was very hesitant but kind, following closely behind Trooper, who was being led around the arena by Kirsty. Within 15 minutes Battle had his very first trot; it was remarkable how far he'd come in the time he had been with us. Battle continued to make progress over the next week, and was soon loading on the truck and being taken for his first ride on the beach, having his very first canter and jumping over a small log in the forest. Trooper came too but was a little lame, so Kirsty just led him. It was impossible not to smile as we watched her run down the length of the beach with the young stallion cantering alongside her. She was experiencing a lot of joy from handling this gorgeous pony, and considered herself very lucky to have the opportunity to train him.

With Battle making such rapid progress Vicki was optimistic that he would be ready for the first Stallion Challenges two months later, but just when things were looking promising he developed an abscess and went lame. Since both of the new stallions were now unable to be ridden, we used the time to get them gelded and have their teeth done. Trooper was just four years old and Battle eight — much younger than the previous trainer had estimated.

WE HAD AN ADVENTURE DOWN SOUTH PLANNED with the horses for a week later, and Amanda was hoping to have one of her Kaimanawas ready to ride. Between her three boys, Amanda was having a rough time of it and was almost at the point of quitting; she frequently claimed that if she heard the word 'Kaimanawa' just one more time she'd scream. Hoping to take some of the pressure off her, Vicki offered to take over Tullock's training permanently, and Amanda quickly agreed. Right now Amanda desperately needed to save her courage and energy for Nikau and Hoff — her two challenge horses.

Obviously Hoff wasn't an option for the adventure, so Amanda caught Nikau and checked him over, as she'd done countless times during the

Top
Kirsty and Spotlight (at front), and Amanda and Nikau galloping through the estuary at high tide.

Bottom
Elder and I walking through the channel, with Kirsty and Spotlight in the background.

past month. For the first time, he didn't react at all to pressure on his withers and she felt enormous relief. Although she hadn't been able to ride him for the past four weeks, she had spent her time with him wisely — he could now load on the horse float, which was one of the requirements for the halter element of the Stallion Challenges, and she'd also taught him to paw the air on command and come when she whistled.

She tied Nikau up, and began saddling him; he swished his tail and stamped a hoof in annoyance. Patting him reassuringly, she led him out onto the arena — but when she asked him to trot on the lunge he took off bucking across the arena. There was nothing enticing about mounting him, and a disheartened Amanda led him back to the stables. Vicki soon convinced her that she'd given up too quickly, however, and with our trip down south now only days away Amanda turned Nikau around and stood him beside the mounting block. Leaning her weight on him, she soon got him used to the feel of a rider again. Feeling a little more optimistic, she took him back to the arena for a walk and he didn't put a foot wrong.

The next morning dawned clear, and Nikau was loaded on the truck with five of the showjumpers and Elder — if Nikau could cope with a group ride at the beach, Amanda was confident that he would be fine to go south. The ride started well; Amanda followed the other horses down the track to the beach, gaining confidence stride by stride. By the time they reached the estuary she felt safe enough to trot, and Nikau felt steady beneath her.

It was the first time we had taken the horses to the beach at high tide, and we quickly discovered the enjoyment of it. Making the most of the estuary being under water, we didn't even try the ocean beach; instead, the girls cantered through the shallow water while Elder and I watched from the shore. Elder kept inching closer to the water's edge and, realising he'd love a swim, I led him out to the deep channel and joined the other horses, trying to convince myself that the winter chill and freezing water was warmer than it felt.

Galloping through the shallow waters quickly instilled further confidence in Amanda, and she decided that Nikau was ready to try his first jump. Following the showjumpers into the forest, they rode over to a felled tree and one by one cantered around and jumped over the log. When it was Amanda's turn, she trotted Nikau up to it and he gathered his legs and jumped the log with plenty of room to spare. Smiling, she leant over and gave him a pat. Considering that this was only his third ride under saddle, it had gone far better than Amanda had expected and she was excited to see how he would be on our southern adventure.

The following day Anzac and I also had our first ride since I'd been bitten. After six weeks I could finally straighten my arm, and although it was still stiff and sore I wasn't going to miss out on all the fun.

TOP
Elder watching Nikau and the
showjumpers play in the water.

BOTTOM
A perfect end to a great ride.

CHAPTER 12

The Wild West

Riding out in the snow near the Kaimanawa Ranges, not far from where the horses were mustered.

For my birthday we were going snowboarding at Mount Ruapehu, and had decided to extend the trip and take some Kaimanawas with us. Over the past few years we had begun the tradition of doing some sort of adventurous activity on our birthdays — instead of presents — and since mine fell in the middle of winter, it normally involved snow. Riding horses in the snow was something we had always dreamed about, but since we live in the 'winterless north' we had never had the chance to do it. This would be an adventure for both us and the horses.

On our way to the mountain we were spending a night at Mellonsfolly Ranch, an authentic Wild West town near Raetihi, and were especially excited to be meeting Tommy Waara there. He was one of our fellow trainers in the Stallion Challenges and was bringing his two Kaimanawas, Tukotahi and Te One, to show us the best trails to ride on. It was an eight-hour drive to the ranch, so we stopped overnight in Cambridge to rest the horses. The next morning, Vicki and Amanda drove ahead with the horses while I went with a friend in a ute. The extra vehicle was needed because only some of us were staying down south to go snowboarding while the rest were driving the horses home early.

We left before sunrise. Three hours later, as the sun rose, I looked around in puzzlement. I didn't recognise any landmarks, and I'd driven this road countless times each winter. We typed our destination into the GPS, and it said we were five hours away from Mellonsfolly Ranch; I was confused. By my calculations we should have been almost there, so I re-checked. Again the GPS said five hours, and then out the window I saw a sign saying 'New Plymouth 20 km' — in horror it dawned on us that we had missed the turn-off to the national park and were hundreds of kilometres from where we were supposed to be.

Calling Vicki, I explained the dilemma and, laughing at our stupidity, she asked if there was a short-cut through the mountains to save us time backtracking — the film crew was waiting for us and there was work to be done. After a bit of research we found a road and, hoping it would save us some time, turned off onto it — completely unprepared for the one-lane gravel roads, sheer cliffs, hair-pin turns and slips along what we later discovered is known as the Forgotten Highway. It wasn't until we found wandering cattle, horses and billy goats on the road that we realised how seldom this road was used, but by then we had lost cell-phone reception and had no way of knowing how much further we still had to go — or even if we were on the right road. Eventually we did get back to civilisation, and with relief turned back onto the main state highway. The mountain pass had saved us over an hour of driving, and although we were still hours behind schedule at least we had survived the rough country roads.

If we'd thought the Forgotten Highway was bad, however, it was nothing in comparison to the final stretch of road leading down to Mellonsfolly Ranch! It was obvious where Vicki had driven the truck, because there were tyre tracks imprinted in the loose gravel that had slipped over the road. When the entrance to the Wild West town finally came into view, we were relieved; it had been a long drive with our added detour, and we were keen to start exploring. The place was far more authentic than we could have imagined, and we quickly fell in love with its genuine feel — when we pulled up, everyone was dressed in Western clothes and we watched in amusement as Amanda lassoed Paula. It felt as though we'd fallen backwards into another time and place where cowgirls and cowboys roamed the Wild West and wild horses were commonplace.

Now that we'd arrived, we all caught the horses and got them ready to ride; the Kaimanawas suited their Western saddles. Getting into the spirit of things, we led our Stallion Challenges horses down the main street and had a stand-off in front of the saloon with Tommy and Te One; it wasn't serious, though, and introductions were quickly made. It was special meeting another Kaimanawa with his owner, and watching how Tommy interacted with his horses was very telling — the trust his horses had in him was absolute and they were obviously enjoying their new life with him.

Lunch was now ready, so we hitched our horses to the rails and headed inside to eat. Even the food was authentic, and the owners of the ranch were dressed to look the part. By early afternoon we were itching to ride, so the girls swapped their Western saddles for English ones — old habits die hard. I jumped on Anzac bareback with just a halter, since he

TOP
Amanda and Nikau having
some bonding time at
Mellonsfolly Ranch.

BOTTOM
Amanda lassoing Makaila
on Spotlight.

was still unfamiliar with the girth and bit.

Tommy led the way and we enjoyed the scenery, soon heading up a steep bush track towards a lookout point. After climbing at altitude for almost an hour I was wishing I had a saddle on, because I knew that the ride back down would be just as long. Once we got to the top the ground flattened out a little, and we cantered along the tracks. It was hard to believe that less than three months previously five of the eight horses on the ride had been wild stallions in the Kaimanawa Ranges — anyone seeing them now certainly wouldn't have believed it.

Te One and Argo were in the front, and both were bold and brave. Vicki and Tommy often left the track to jump up and down banks or weave through trees, and Tommy even hacked branches down with a machete to clear the path. Even Nikau, who had been ridden the least, strode out well, and Amanda was thoroughly enjoying riding him on the steep hill country. This kind of ride is often the making of horses, and being on the road, loading and unloading, covering and uncovering, bandaging and being caught gives them an extensive, yet fun, learning experience.

The ride back down was a little more challenging. I quickly discovered that, like many young horses, Anzac had no concept of how to walk down hills. Navigating the steepest parts bareback with just a halter proved hazardous and there was many a time when I almost slipped over his neck; it was a struggle to stay on. We made it back without any casualties, though, and settled the horses down before heading inside for bubble-baths, dinner, a game of billiards and talking around the campfire.

THE NEXT MORNING WE WOKE AT DAWN for target shooting. Amanda was quite impressed with her accuracy until I hit the targets with nine out of my 10 bullets! Vicki was by far the worst shot, and quickly got impatient and left to catch the horses. Saddling up, we had one last canter down the main street of the Wild West town while Amanda made a nuisance of herself, lassoing riders as they went past.

We were having so much fun that we would have loved to have stayed for a few more days, but the snow was beckoning. We were equally excited about riding the horses at the base of the Kaimanawa Ranges, not far from where they had been mustered. The alpine landscape was barren, with pockets of snow clinging to crevices and a freezing-cold wind coming straight off the mountain. Snow swirled around us as we got the horses ready, but only added to the novelty of the experience. We soon realised that we were underdressed, and darted back into the truck to layer up with snow gear. However, once we began moving, we barely noticed the wintery conditions.

This time Tommy rode his bay stallion Tukotahi, and our friend Sarah rode Te One. Vicki, Amanda and I were on our challenge horses, and Memo and Remembrance, two of our mares from the 2012 muster, were also on the ride, with the last horse to join us being Spotlight, Vicki's palomino. It was beautiful country to ride over; the rocky outcrops, windswept cliffs and plant life are unique to the central plateau. As we rode, the Kaimanawas tugged the reins out of our hands so that they could eat certain shrubs and tussocks; they were so eager that we nicknamed the plants Kaimanawa Kandy. Spotlight, our only domestic-born horse, wasn't interested. We even tried to hand-feed him the plants, but he turned his head away in distaste.

Fortunately the snow didn't cover every inch of ground, as the rocks were quite difficult to navigate and it would have been dangerous riding in terrain with the footing obscured. There was just enough to enjoy, however, and when we found fresh powder the Kaimanawas pawed the snow and Argo even lay down while Vicki sat on him. These were the conditions the Kaimanawas were used to in the Ranges, and they were in their element; surefooted and fearless as they powered through rivers, down banks and over snow-drifts.

Vicki, Amanda and I branched away from the others, carefully making our way through the rocks, and dropped down into an old riverbed. The fine gravel surface was perfect for a canter and we urged the horses forward, weaving along the scoured-out path that would rage with water during the spring snow melts. In front of us, Vicki took her hands off the reins and spread her arms as if she were flying, and Amanda and I followed suit. In that moment we felt freer than ever before, and the

Top
The Kaimanawas enjoying the snow, not far from where they were mustered.

Bottom
Argo, Nikau and Anzac cantering down a dry riverbed.

Top
Falling off Anzac while trying to scale a steep cliff back into the riverbed.

Bottom
Amanda and I love snowboarding with friends — it's one of our favourite things to do in winter.

horses remained steady beneath us. As we rounded the bend we came to a rocky area that descended; it was a dried-up waterfall. Turning the horses, we jumped up the steep banks to the side and navigated our way around it; to get back down to the riverbed, we now had a huge cliff to negotiate.

Vicki went first on Argo and they slid down, making it safely to the bottom. It was far steeper and higher than anything we had previously attempted, and I hesitantly followed in their hoof-prints. Anzac leapt off the ledge, and instead of sliding down rocked forward into a canter — I flipped over his head, somersaulting to the ground before regaining my footing. Doubled over laughing, I forgot to catch Anzac, and by the time I turned around he had already re-scaled the cliff and was standing waiting beside Nikau. The cliff was almost vertical and with every step I risked sliding to the bottom. Finally, I was able to dig my boots into the rock enough to gain traction and inched my way to the top. Amanda attempted the descent next and, like Vicki, she made it safely down; not willing to repeat my mistake, I led Anzac over the edge and together we slid down, arriving at the bottom in fine style.

Joining back up with the others, we all swapped ponies so that people could have a turn on others, and I handed the reins to our friend Makaila. Anzac was still quite funny with strangers, but Makaila was one of his favourite people and he behaved beautifully for the rest of the ride as they went in search of deeper snow and more dramatic landscapes.

By midday, the weather had worsened considerably and everyone returned to load up so that Vicki could travel north with the horses. The rest of us were heading up the mountain for the next few days to go snowboarding, and we couldn't wait; there was plenty of fresh powder expected overnight and the next day was supposed to be a bluebird day on the mountain. After three intensive months working with the wild Kaimanawas, it was a relief to get away from horses and spend some time hanging out with friends. In fact, we enjoyed it so much that we returned a week later to go snowboarding again, and on our way home went black-water rafting at Waitomo Caves.

Only three months after the muster,
Argo would lie down on voice command.

CHAPTER 13

Classrooms and playgrounds

Nikau and Amanda
jumping down by the river.

Once back at home we stepped things up a notch: it was time for the Kaimanawas to focus on their training for the first leg of the Stallion Challenges, the Major Milestone at Equidays. There was plenty for them to learn. The Major Milestone had two classes — the ridden which was under saddle, and the halter where the horses were presented on the lead. Both were freestyles, which meant we could decide what to include in each workout, and this suited us well. Since it was so early in the horses' training it was best to focus on what they were naturally good at, rather than force them into a predetermined mould.

Up to this point formal training hadn't been a priority for our Kaimanawas. Our focus had simply been for them to enjoy life so that they would transition to domestication with the maximum happiness. For a wild horse, every day involves learning — fences, water troughs, cars, trucks, saddles, bridles and riders are all things they have to become accustomed to — but schooling on a contact (in a bridle, i.e. working on the bit) or getting them used to a competition environment wasn't something we had done yet.

Vicki's new stallion Battle had a lot to learn in a very short time, but now that he was sound again he was slowly gaining mileage. By Equidays he would have been with us for only 10 weeks so Vicki had very low expectations for him. His workout in both the halter and ridden classes would be as basic as possible, but she was pleased with how well he was coming along and was confident that he would be ready to compete.

Meanwhile our three main boys, Nikau, Anzac and Argo, were gaining a unique set of skills and we began to focus on how we would showcase these. A few weeks after we returned from the snow, Amanda decided to school Nikau over jumps for the first time. He'd already jumped over logs and ditches and up and down banks, but this was his first time over coloured poles. He was unsure what was expected of him at first, and he trotted towards the first crossbar and jumped it hesitantly. The second time he was much more confident, and within a few days he was jumping over 90-centimetre oxers and a dinghy. Nikau's technique was very correct and Amanda was pleased; she loved producing young showjumpers and was looking forward to watching him develop — her horse had the talent, now he just needed the mileage.

Hoping that Anzac would be just as talented, I took him over some jumps — and it was quickly obvious that he lacked any natural technique or scope whatsoever. Laughing, I held my head in my hands in despair; either I was a terrible trainer or my pony seemed to have no particular talent. At this stage the only thing going for him was how quiet he was for kids to handle and ride, so I spent a lot of time with Mouse, incorporating her into his workout for the ridden class; soon she could walk, trot and canter Anzac under saddle by herself.

Anzac and I also mastered the art of bareback and bridleless work, and I was very proud about what I'd accomplished — of the three of us, I was the only one who hadn't successfully trained a horse to be ridden this way, and for me it was a very rewarding process. Initially I had been very nervous about training a wild stallion, but every day I was exceeding my own expectations. Deciding to teach Anzac to bow, I spent some time with him working on this. Within 15 minutes he was bending his leg and lowering into the bowing position, so I fed him and put him away for the night. The next day, he performed a perfectly executed bow.

Argo was, of course, the most advanced of the three horses and had mastered a range of skills, including pulling a cart — but Vicki had even bigger plans for him. Over the years she had taught a number of horses to work bareback and bridleless, with just a rope around the neck to guide them, and she decided that Argo could do one better — he could work completely at liberty.

Always a quick learner, Argo soon got the hang of it, turning when Vicki used her hands to direct his movement and stopping when she shifted her weight back. By day 110 after the muster he was working to voice commands and Vicki could canter him down the beach with no gear to guide him. Although she didn't always have complete control, it was impressive to watch — we had no doubt that with a little more time this would be an impressive display of horsemanship.

Argo was also the bravest and most willing young horse we had encountered — he would go onto, over or under anything Vicki asked him to. On rides they were always leaving the beaten track in search

Argo lying down
on command.

of adventure, and one time at the beach he jumped up onto a floating platoon, balancing carefully as it rocked on the water beneath; he showed complete trust in Vicki. One of Argo's favourite things to do was to lie down in the sand. Every time he went to the beach Vicki allowed this, and each time she said the word *down*. Hoping that he'd associated the word *down* with lying down, she stood him in pile of sawdust at home and tried to teach him to lie down on voice command. Amanda and I were very sceptical about it working. After watching her repeat the word *down* and point to the ground for half an hour with no success, we left — and no sooner had we turned our backs than he dropped to the ground. Vicki called us back in excitement, and we couldn't quite believe our eyes! Asking him to stand, she again told him to lie down and this time it only took a few minutes for him to do so. She had successfully taught her horse to lie down without using the traditional method of tying or holding up a leg and tipping the horse off balance — we were quite in awe.

On day 114 we took Anzac and Nikau to their first practice competition. Both Amanda and I were unsure how the ponies would cope in such a different environment, or with jumping over new fences. Both had only jumped a couple of times at home, but it was a good opportunity to get them used to new places. When we arrived, the horses were surprisingly settled. I saddled Anzac up and rode to the ring for the 50-centimetre class. Although reasonably relaxed, he was worried about the edge of the arena and was nervous working against the fence line; our own arena didn't have a fence, so I made a note to work on this aspect before Equidays.

In the first class his jumping was better than expected, and although he'd shown very little talent at home I was impressed with the scope he showed over some of the fences — yes, he was green and unsure; but he was also willing and honest and I quickly revised my earlier opinion. He had some serious talent for jumping, and I needed to incorporate this into my workout for the challenges.

Soon it was Nikau and Amanda's turn, and she started getting him ready. As she lifted the saddle onto his back, he tensed and half-reared.

Since he was tied to a post-and-rail fence there was nowhere for him to go, so he rocked back on his hindquarters and jumped the fence from a stand-still. Shocked, Amanda dropped the saddle onto the rails and vaulted over the fence to calm Nikau down and see what was wrong with him. Running her hands gently over him, she checked him and when she got to his withers he started trembling violently. Reaching forward, she gave him a pat and he quickly relaxed. Nikau's wither abscess had obviously returned, and Amanda was disheartened. He had been going so well and shown so much promise for Equidays, and now he would have to have more time off to recover.

Hoping that she could use the spare time to win Hoff over, Amanda began working with him again. His disposition had improved slightly since his teeth had been done, but he was still untrustworthy. Not a day went by when he didn't threaten to bite her, but her perseverance was beginning to pay off. She was finally able to lead him without a fence separating them for safety, although she didn't feel confident touching him unless there was something between them as a precaution.

Finally, four months after the muster, Amanda felt that Hoff was ready to go to the beach for the first time and she set about teaching him to load. Going up the ramp was no problem, but once in the confines of the truck with him Amanda was very careful to keep well away from both his teeth and his hind legs to avoid being bitten or kicked. Finally, she managed to get him tied up and the divider closed. It was a massive breakthrough that she felt confident enough to lead him at the beach, since he was still very unpredictable; most of the way Amanda walked backwards so that she could keep a careful eye on him. When they waded into the ocean with the other horses, the girls on shore joked that Hoff had returned to his natural environment, and when I asked what they meant they admitted that they had nicknamed him *The Shark*. In fact he had a lot of nicknames — on a good day Amanda called him *Hoffle Poff* and on his worst days he was still referred to as *The Hoff Burger*. He still had a long way to go before we could trust him, and we were unsure whether he would ever be a horse you could turn your back on without fear of being attacked.

Top
Amanda jumping Viking for the public during our book launch.

Bottom
Anzac bowing with Mouse.

WITH ONLY A MONTH TO GO until Equidays, the horses were given a diverse combination of schooling and adventures. The arena was their classroom, and every time we schooled them it was important that they learnt something new or improved in some way. Since formal schooling was foreign to the Kaimanawas, we made sure that these lessons were enjoyable — as soon as anything got too repetitive, the horses, like little kids at school, switched off and become bored, especially Argo who, at only three years old, had a baby brain and got distracted easily.

Very rarely did the Kaimanawas get more than 25 minutes of arena work, and no more than a couple of times a week. The rest of the time we took them on adventures: the beach, forest, river and farm were their playground. During these rides our sole purpose was to have fun; they were always ridden on the buckle (with very loose reins) and we never expected them to learn new things. It was an opportunity for the horses to mentally and physically relax, explore and simply enjoy life. The basics were non-negotiable, of course — they were expected to go in straight lines at the correct speed, for example, but apart from that they were simply allowed to be horses and this kept them engaged and happy. We've always done the same with our showjumpers — they work on the arena a couple of times each week and have equal amounts of playtime. The fun stuff keeps them fit and fresh, and it's hugely beneficial in the competition arena to have horses that are switched on and enjoying life rather than shut down and going through the motions.

The final thing the Kaimanawas needed to experience before Equidays was large crowds, so we organised a launch for my first book, *For the Love of Horses*, which was due out in bookstores in early October. The weather on launch day was miserable, but in between the wind and rain we enjoyed some clear blue skies and the horses behaved well. With objects blowing in every direction and hundreds of people watching, it really was a worst-case scenario for the horses; and, although it wasn't ideal conditions for the gathered public, it did set the horses up well for the Stallion Challenges. After *that* they would be ready for anything!

Argo was a star, working at liberty through all his paces and then jumping over a small wall — to say that people were impressed would be an understatement. Anzac was also sweet and willing, and walked and trotted with Mouse and bowed for the crowd. When it was my turn to ride him, we started well but, partway through our workout, a gust of wind blew all the jumps over and gave both of us a fright. Anzac was quick to settle, though, and worked bareback and bridleless although it took a little effort — he was much more interested in eating the grass!

Nikau also made an appearance, even though he'd only been ridden twice in the past month; if he wanted to have any hope of coping at Equidays he needed to have these life experiences. When we started saddling up, people had already gathered around the yards and Nikau was unsettled and kicked one of the girls who was helping to saddle him. Once mounted he was still tense, so Amanda took him further back, away from the crowd, and worked him in the distance until he settled down.

At the end of the demonstration we invited the crowd to come forward and meet the horses. Within seconds, Anzac and Argo were lost in a sea of people and we quickly realised we had worded our offer to greet the horses poorly. We should have given more precise instructions. We'd expected people to walk forward and approach the horses' heads — some did, but others had their hands on the horses' backs and kids were even grabbing at their legs. Just because the horses were quiet for us to handle and ride didn't mean that it was safe for dozens of strangers to mob them; they were still recently mustered horses and the public's level of naïvety about formerly wild horses amazed us. Worried, Vicki and I kept a careful eye on Argo and Anzac's body language to make sure they weren't getting unsettled. We needn't have worried, though, as the horses loved the attention. Seeing what was happening, Amanda led Nikau well back and only let people come forward one at a time to greet him — with him having already kicked one person that day, she didn't want anyone else injured. He thoroughly enjoyed meeting the people, however, lowering his head to greet young children and standing quietly while the adults patted him on the forehead or neck.

Soon it was time to put the horses away, and we headed inside for a reading and book-signings.

CHAPTER 14

Major Milestone

Amanda and Nikau
dressed as ferals
during their freestyle
performance in the
Major Milestone.
TUImages

In the final days leading up to Equidays, we realised just how unprepared we were — another two weeks of training would have been hugely beneficial. But, rather than overload the horses in the last 10 days, we backed right off their schooling, instead cantering out over the hills and swimming at the beach. It was too late to teach them new things at this point; Nikau, Anzac, Argo and even Battle (who'd had only half the amount of work) were very well-adjusted horses, and overwhelming them in the final hours would only stress them out and decrease their chances of giving a polished performance in the ring.

On the Monday before the event, we ran through the horses' routines and timed the workouts to ensure that they were within the time allocation. Argo and Anzac worked well — the best they ever had. We were very proud of the horses and how much they had learnt. Vicki and I were sure that they had a good shot at being in the top three if everything went well on the day. Nikau and Battle were a little more unpredictable, and Amanda and Vicki weren't confident about their chances — the only goal with them was not to fall off.

We knew that it was unlikely the horses would perform as well at Equidays as they did at home. The atmosphere would be different from anything they had encountered and there was a high chance that they would be tense, although we had done everything possible to acclimatise them. Our goal had been to produce happy and relaxed horses that were enjoying their new lives in domestication, and all the Kaimanawas we had competing in the Major Milestone were indeed well adjusted; regardless of how they performed, we were proud of them.

Hoff was the only other horse eligible for the Stallion Challenges, but there was no way he could attend — not even for the halter class. He just wasn't safe enough to handle, and if he got loose we couldn't trust him not to hurt anyone. Growing up, we'd read books and watched movies about rogue stallions that couldn't be tamed, and now we were beginning to question whether Hoff would ever be safely domesticated.

The drive to Equidays was long, and we left at dawn so that we would have plenty of time to settle the horses after the five-hour journey — we had four Kaimanawas and five showjumpers with us. When we arrived, we hopped on the Kaimanawas for a ride, strolling around the grounds to get them used to the hustle and bustle of one of New Zealand's largest equestrian events. As expected, Argo was bold and brave, and strode out confidently, but Nikau and Anzac were a little more timid and pressed close to each other, unsure about the cars, trucks and trade stands that were scattered around the showgrounds; as was Battle, who was on the lead. Returning to the truck, we washed all the horses and rugged them before putting them in yards for the night. Once they were settled, we headed to the seminar room for a Trainers and Clinicians briefing, then cleaned our gear and laid out our costumes for the following morning.

We woke at sunrise to feed the horses, and at 7.30 am we saddled up; we had a 15-minute slot to get them used to the arena, and the horses desperately needed it. Although unsure at first, Argo and Nikau soon relaxed and worked well, but Anzac never truly settled, shying away from the signage at the edges of the arena. Returning to the truck, I gave him a reassuring pat. I knew that he wasn't ready for the first class, which was in less than an hour, but there was nothing more I could do to prepare him. Knowing that Anzac's workout was unlikely to go well, I let go of all my expectations of him — whatever he gave me in the ring would have to be good enough.

It was completely understandable that he was so worried — nothing in his wild life could have prepared him for today. Many of the other horses in the competition were also a little unsure, and a few of the trainers were adapting their workouts to simplify the routines. The atmosphere between the trainers was surprisingly relaxed; for the most part there was no competitive rivalry. All the training had been done at home, and now it would come down to the best horse on the day. The focus seemed to be on the breed in general, rather than on winning, and all the trainers were pleased at how far their horses had come; they had formed a genuine bond with their horses and were proud to showcase them as ambassadors of the breed.

The first event, the CopRice Ridden Freestyle, soon started, and the first horse entered the ring. Anzac and I were second, and I warmed him up carefully. He was relaxed and jumping well but still unsure about

Anzac working bareback and bridleless during his freestyle.
Kimber Brown

Top
Amanda dressed as a feral, with Vicki dressed as Mary Poppins in the background.
Kimber Brown

Bottom
Battle and Vicki during their freestyle.
Kimber Brown

— 166 —

the edges of the arena, so I made sure that my props were set up well away from the fences, which were crowded with more than a thousand spectators. After this morning I'd been unsure whether Anzac would behave for Mouse, but we'd spent so much time practising that Mouse deserved to be a part of this. At home she'd been confident cantering and jumping on her own, but today I ran alongside Anzac to keep him relaxed and we changed the routine slightly so that she wouldn't have to canter him. Mouse sat quietly on him at the gateway and when the bell rang we entered the ring, then walked over the see-saw and trotted over a jump, while the wings of our butterfly outfits flapped in time to his movements, before finally stepping up onto the wooden box.

As Mouse slid over Anzac's rump and dropped to the ground I undid the girth, removed the saddle and vaulted onto him bareback to complete our performance — jumping a small oxer, soaring over a 90-centimetre wall and then going from a canter to a halt. Leaning forward, I removed Anzac's bridle and passed it to Mouse; then, with just a rope to guide him, I jumped the oxer again and did another canter-to-halt transition before walking back over the see-saw and exiting the arena. Smiling, I gave Anzac a pat — although he'd been worried by all the things around him, he'd done everything asked of him and I was proud of how he'd coped under pressure.

Amanda was waiting on the sidelines, holding Nikau; she'd been dreading this day for weeks. With so little mileage under saddle, because of Nikau's abscess, he was one of the most inexperienced horses in the class. There were only four horses until her turn, so she mounted and began warming him up; to her relief, he was relaxed and attentive. Both Amanda and Nikau had skeletons painted on them, and feathers and beads in their hair; it made a striking picture as they entered the ring, the white bones clear against his dark coat.

They started well, with simple walk, trot and canter transitions, and although Nikau was obviously green he was very willing. Halting in front of the judges, he pawed on command and side-passed (this involves the horse moving sideways, crossing one leg over the other with no forward or backward motion), before picking up a canter again and approaching the first jump. He hesitated slightly on take-off, but cleared it well. Turning, Amanda and Nikau approached the vertical while helpers raised the height of the first jump. The oxer now stood at 95 centimetres, and Nikau cantered in and jumped it with perfect technique. Giving him a pat, Amanda slowed him to a walk before saluting the judges. Without a doubt, those four minutes in the ring had been Nikau's best behaved ever under saddle, and Amanda was beaming. He'd had to overcome a lot to be there that day, and she couldn't have been more pleased.

Next to go was Vicki on Battle, and as expected he was hesitant and wobbly; he'd only had 10 weeks of handling and it was a huge accomplishment to even have him at the show — only 11 of the 19 horses originally entered in the challenge were competing in the ridden class. As she exited the arena, Vicki was happy with how Battle had worked — he would undoubtedly place last, but it had been a positive experience for him and would be a good stepping stone towards the final challenge at the Horse of the Year show in another five months.

Vicki quickly returned to the truck, got dressed in her Mary Poppins outfit and mounted Argo, who was saddled up and waiting. As she returned to the arena, there was huge applause; Paddy Mair had just done an impressive workout on his horse Kachina, and was by far the one to beat. He'd obviously been joking the night before when he'd said his horse had only been ridden a handful of times and not to expect too much.

Soon it was Argo's turn. Vicki entered the ring, holding an umbrella, to the song 'A Spoonful of Sugar'. Argo was relaxed and working kindly until a huge gust of wind blew through, causing Vicki's umbrella to turn inside out. Giving him a pat, Vicki continued but Argo's focus was divided and, although he did everything he was asked, he understandably wasn't as soft and relaxed as usual. Halting him, Vicki handed the umbrella to a helper, then leant forward and removed the bridle.

With Argo working completely at liberty, they performed flawless flying changes, 10-metre circles, and even jumped and climbed on obstacles, with just the slightest aids from Vicki. Drawing Argo to a halt, she gave him the command to lie down, but just as he began pawing the ground the bell sounded — anything after the time limit wouldn't be scored, so she saluted the judges and exited the arena. All that time training him to lie down had been wasted for the want of 10 seconds. While the routine hadn't gone like clockwork, the fact that Argo had coped when everything had fallen to pieces at the beginning was a true testament to his character.

All the horses returned to the arena for the prize-giving and their results were called out in reverse order from tenth to first place. As we waited in line for the place-getters to be announced, Argo lay down on command between the other horses, watching alertly when Amanda and Nikau stepped forward to receive eighth place and Anzac and I went forward to collect fifth. Soon just the top two horses remained: they had been notably more advanced than all the others, and we were unsure what order they would place in. Finally, Argo was called forward as the runner-up and Kachina was crowned the winner.

CHAPTER 15

Dark horse

Vicki and Levado competing in the Grand
Prix Derby, where they finished seventh.

Top
Amanda and Viking competing in the Grand Prix Derby, where they placed eighth.

Bottom
Vicki and Premier placed second in the Derby.

The following day was more relaxing for the Kaimanawas, as they had a day off before the halter class. Because these horses had such a huge public following, a 'Meet and Greet' had been organised and we led our Kaimanawas over to meet their fans. It was a great opportunity for the trainers to introduce their horses, and the quieter ones were all led forward for people to pat over the fence. Anzac, Argo and Tommy Waara's grey, Te One, were all safe with kids and we called children forward from the crowd to go for a ride on them — it was the highlight of their weekend. Many of the people watching felt invested in the horses, having watched their progress on social media ever since the muster. It amazed us just how many people were lining up to see the Kaimanawas.

As soon as the Meet and Greet finished, Amanda and Vicki rushed off to mount their showjumpers, who were saddled and waiting at the ring for the Grand Prix Derby event. The Derby was technical and the fences were imposing, especially for showjumpers who weren't used to jumping cross-country fences. Some of the nation's best horse-and-rider combinations were competing and, of the dozens of starters, three of our horses finished the first round in the top 10 and returned to jump a shortened course against the clock.

Vicki had the only horse that went clear in the first round and had four faults in hand. All she had to do was finish clear and the win would be hers, but if she dropped a rail she would then have to have the fastest time to keep the lead. Hoping for a clear round, Vicki carefully guided Premier around the course, but he slipped coming into the white oxer and knocked a rail down, dropping them to second place. Vicki also placed seventh on Levado, and Amanda on Viking was eighth.

The next morning dawned clear and we began preparing the Kaimanawas for their final event, the Thoroughbred Floats Halter Class: the most prestigious class of the weekend, with $10,000 on offer. Wanting the horses to look their best, Vicki and I groomed them until their coats gleamed with health. Then, looking around, we noticed that Nikau was still in his yard and Amanda was nowhere in sight. We found her sleeping in the truck. When she realised she'd slept in, she jumped up and rushed outside to groom her horse. Stressed, and worried that she hadn't done enough to prepare for the halter class, she began teaching Nikau new tricks; apparently, she had decided that what she'd practised at home wouldn't be enough for a decent placing. Her secret weapon had been Nikau coming to her whistle, but since the halter class was being held on a grass arena there was no way he would listen — instead, he'd just eat. With only an hour to go until we were due at the ring, she started gathering umbrellas and random things to get Nikau used to them, frantically trying to come up with something new.

Nikau was a little confused and wary of all that was suddenly being asked of him, but in general he was quite accepting. Vicki watched, and decided that Argo could also use the last half-hour to get used to new things; she got him walking under a tarpaulin and over different objects. I, however, decided to stick with what we knew — the practice we had put in at home was enough and I was confident that Anzac would hold his own in the most important class of the weekend.

Soon it was competition time, and we led our horses to the ring. Amanda was the second to go. On the sidelines, Vicki and I stood unbelieving as he went through his workout — no one would have guessed that he'd only practised it for the first time an hour beforehand. When they reached the Thoroughbred Float, in which he was to load, Amanda let Nikau loose and then walked onto the ramp and whistled. At the command he ignored the tempting grass and self-loaded perfectly — it was very impressive, and better than any of their practices. When we commented on it later, she laughed and said that she'd been holding a handful of feed — so of course he had come to her. The judges, whose view was obscured, wouldn't have known and we gave her credit for the ingenious idea.

Next in was Argo. His workout started well; he was strapped into a harness and pulled his props into the ring, then climbed up onto 1-metre-high steps so that Vicki could vault on him and slide off his back. Next he balanced on a swaying bridge, walked under a billowing tarpaulin, trotted on the lead, picked up all four hooves and loaded well on the float. For the most part he was relaxed, but the additional manoeuvres Vicki had

Top
Anzac taking off during
his performance in
the halter class.

Middle
Nikau placed runner-up
in the Thoroughbred
Floats Halter Class.

Bottom
Equidays is a big event
for us and requires many
people behind the scenes,
including the film crew.

Top
Argo galloping around the arena at liberty during the night show, where the
top four Kaimanawas from the Ridden Freestyle were showcased.

Bottom
Vicki and Premier competing in the Grand Prix Derby during the night show.
TUImages

— 176 —

added in at the last minute had made him a little tense and worried — sometimes it's best to stick with what you know. Vicki was disappointed; she knew that the errors they had made were due to changing the routine at the last minute and she was sorry she'd let the horse down. Argo was more than capable of winning, and a poor judgement call on her behalf had jeopardised his chances.

Anzac's turn was fast approaching, and I was torn by indecision. I had trained him to work with just a rope around his neck, but after watching one of the other trainers lose control when working their Kaimanawa at liberty I was unsure whether this was worth the risk — perhaps it would be better to be safe and use a halter. Hoping that my faith in Anzac wasn't misguided, I decided to stick with the original plan and we entered the ring. Like when we had trained, he worked through the obstacles, jumped over ribbons and then walked, trotted and cantered alongside me, although he missed his cue to slow down and it was obvious to the judges that he wasn't listening as well as he should have been. Next I led Anzac over and under obstacles before approaching the float. When I asked him to load he hesitated a little before walking into the narrow, confined space. Before he was completely in, he panicked and rushed backwards; there was a moment when I feared that I'd lost him completely, but rather than bolting off he paused at the base of the ramp and waited for me to catch him — and then loaded perfectly. To finish off, I asked him to bow in front of the judges, and again he missed his cue, putting his head down to graze — although he got it right the second time. Laughing, I led him from the ring, and with a rueful shake of my head admitted that a halter could have come in handy.

The last of our horses to compete was Battle. Vicki took a cautious approach, attempting only the most basic of performances. There were marks available for catching an unhaltered horse, but Vicki decided to forfeit these and leave his halter on — he was distracted by everything around him, and she wanted to make things as stress-free for Battle as she could. Next she led him towards the judges, and he stood quietly while she picked up each of his feet; then she walked and trotted him on the lead. The last task she wanted to complete was loading him onto the float.

For the next few minutes, until the final bell rang, she worked quietly with Battle, asking him to load. By the end of her allocated time, Battle only had his front legs on the ramp; but Vicki was happy and led him from the arena with a pat.

While many trainers would have been embarrassed by their horse's lack of skills and not entered the competition, Vicki's attitude was the absolute opposite. She felt that it was important for people to truly appreciate that every horse progresses as an individual, and that some horses take much longer than others. Battle had been basic but willing in both the ridden and the halter classes; if anything, his workouts only emphasised just how advanced the other horses were.

AT THE CONCLUSION OF THE EVENT the trainers led their Kaimanawas into the ring for the prize-giving, and for the three of us it was quite an emotional moment. Without the challenges, all of these horses would have been slaughtered five months earlier and it was remarkable how far they had come in such a short time. Standing side by side, quiet and relaxed, they were incredible ambassadors for the breed and we were grateful to every trainer in the line-up. The time and money they had invested in taming these wild stallions had been extensive, but it had been worth it; the partnership everyone had developed with their horses was obvious.

In reverse order, the horses were called forward to collect their ribbons. Of the 13 horses that had competed in the halter class, Vicki placed sixth, and her overall points meant Argo finished as the Major Milestone Reserve Champion — even with their mistakes it was still a very respectable finish. Anzac was fourth and I gave him a proud pat — he was the only horse in the challenges that had placed in the top five in both classes. Fourth place was announced, then third, and Vicki and I gaped at Amanda — she was either unplaced, which seemed unlikely, or was ranked first or second. After a long moment of anticipation, Amanda's name was called and she was awarded runner-up. With a grin, she led Nikau forward to receive their prize while Vicki and I looked at each other in disbelief. Without her last-minute additions, the original workout she'd planned would have been lucky to have given her a decent placing. We had to give her credit for gaining such high marks; she'd been the dark horse in the competition and had beaten us in convincing style. When Amanda returned to the line-up we congratulated her warmly; there was no denying that it had been an impressive workout and she deserved to finish on such a high after the emotional roller-coaster the Kaimanawas had taken her on.

CHAPTER 16

Down-time

Honor enjoying her months in
the paddock while waiting to foal.

Top
Dancer and I competing
in the Amateur Rider
at Woodhill Sands.

Middle
Amanda and Showtym
Cassanova.

Bottom
Vicki competing
Umhlunga Rock LC in
the 7-Year-Old series.

In the months that followed Equidays, the Stallion Challenges horses took a back seat, enjoying a well-deserved holiday. It was also a chance for us to relax and pursue our other interests in order to mentally recover from the strenuous workload, and also focus on our team of showjumpers. With the filming for the television series now largely complete, it was strange not to have cameras following us around; for the first week we revelled in the novelty of wearing whatever we liked — it felt like Amanda and I didn't get out of our pyjamas for days.

Although we'd had reservations about being filmed, we thoroughly enjoyed the experience and were very lucky that our producer, Rob, had pulled together such a fun team to work with. Dean, our main cameraman, and Esta, our director, had become good friends in the five months since the muster, and the days when they came over were some of our favourite. Having spent hundreds of hours filming, they had seen the horses' progress right from the beginning and had captured most of the highs and lows of their taming. Both were invested in our journey and knew exactly who we were, why we had such a passion for the wild horses, and also had a good understanding of our training methods and philosophies. We were confident that we would be happy with the finished episodes and were looking forward to watching the eight-part series.

Not long after Equidays, Vicki was injured again. A client had withheld information about a young horse Vicki was starting under saddle, and she had been badly injured, re-damaging her wrist and collarbone and causing an old back injury to flare up. Most years we have a team of 12 horses in competition but, since Vicki normally competed most of them, the season became much quieter. Barely able to walk and in agony when she rode, Vicki was advised by the experts to stop riding until her back was sorted, but she refused, eventually settling on a compromise — just riding her three good horses at competitions, while during the week Kirsty and Alexa lunged, swam and rode them. The Grand Prix team — Premier, Cadet and Levado — knew how to jump, so schooling wasn't essential and as long as they maintained their fitness they were on form in the competition arena. A few of the young horses were sold to lighten Vicki's workload, and the rest were turned out onto the hills to rest until Vicki could manage a larger team again.

Vicki had spent years developing a team of horses as promising as her three 'big boys', and to miss the season would have been a shame for horses in their prime. Although she was sore, her injuries didn't affect her results and week after week Vicki came home with wins and placings in the Grand Prix classes. In late October, Premier and Cadet were prepped and ready to compete in their first World Cup — the highest level of showjumping internationally. Levado, who was her most consistent horse, was also performing well and had a convincing lead in the Grand Prix Super Series.

Amanda also had a team of high-quality horses. As well as Showtym Viking, her famed pinto pony, she had two talented five-year-olds and Showtym Cassanova, her 10-year-old pinto gelding, who she was stepping up to World Cup level for the first time. Cassanova had won and placed in Super League classes the season before, and she was confident that he was capable of the biggest heights.

My own season had started well. My favourite mare, Dancer, whom I'd owned for five years, won seven classes at the first four shows of the season. My second horse, Copycat, whom I'd bought the year before when Dancer had been sidelined for several months, was also jumping well, but I was struggling with the workload. Having two showjumpers and two Kaimanawas to work was overwhelming with all of my photography, design and writing commitments; until this year I'd always been a one-horse girl.

In late October, Dancer was kicked on the shoulder by another horse and had to be turned out for 10 weeks. I knew it was a bad sign when, instead of being distressed, I was relieved that I only had one horse to compete again. It was a huge wake-up call for me, and after much discussion with the others I decided to sell Copycat. Vicki tried to talk me out of it, suggesting that I keep him to compete, as he was more talented, and retire Dancer to the broodmare paddock since I wouldn't sell her. I disagreed with her logic, however; Dancer might not be the better horse in some senses, but she was the better horse for me. Unlike my sisters, showjumping was just a hobby for me and my sole focus was to have fun with it.

During the first World Cup show of the season, I stayed at home on foal watch — Showtym Girl, Vicki's prize showjumping mare was due — while Vicki and Amanda headed south to compete. In Vicki's first three classes she was on form, winning the 1.45-metre Speed class on Cadet and placing second on Premier, while Levado won both 1.30-metre classes. The next class was the World Cup itself. With the jumps ranging up to 1.60 metres in height, it was the highest at which Cadet and Cassanova had ever competed, and for Premier it was still a huge ask; he'd only competed a couple of times at that level.

Vicki and Premier were the first to ride, jumping a beautiful round and dropping just one rail. Amanda also had a good ride and Cassanova jumped exceptionally. Next out was Cadet. Everything started well; with every jump he was showing exactly why he deserved to compete against the nation's best horses. With the ninth fence safely behind them and no penalties so far, Vicki approached the third-to-last; but, just when it looked like Cadet might complete the course clear, she miscalculated, riding down the six-stride line in five strides. The horse refused and, not expecting it, Vicki fell hard — re-injuring herself. Limping from the ring, she gave the horse a pat and sat stiffly at the side of the arena to ease the pain in her back.

The top horses were called back to compete in the second round. Amanda entered the ring on Cassanova, ranked in third position, but with the jumps having been raised in height she was nervous and lacked concentration. Early in the course she dropped a rail, and as she approached the oxer, which stood at 1.60 metres, she couldn't see a good take-off distance and circled her horse before slowing him to a walk and saluting to the judge to indicate retirement. Premier was the next to compete and, although she was in agony, Vicki had decided to ride. No one watching from the sidelines would have known Vicki was in pain, though — she rode a faultless round, giving her horse a smooth ride. It was an impressive effort, and Vicki celebrated her first World Cup placing with a finish in fourth place.

With Anzac on holiday, Copycat up for sale and Dancer lame, I had no competition horses to work, so I decided to bring Elder down off the hill and work with him again. It had been over six weeks since he'd been handled and in that time he'd been living a life of leisure, grazing with the Kaimanawa mares. Almost two months had passed since he'd been shod under sedation, and he'd lost a shoe in the paddock and was very lame again. Knowing that his hooves desperately needed some attention, we herded the horses in his paddock down to the home yards.

The mares hadn't been handled for almost three months now, but once haltered they stood to be groomed and have their hooves trimmed. Both Honor and Libby were due to foal; Promise — who'd been brought home weeks earlier — had already given birth to a beautiful chestnut filly which we'd named Secret.

Elder still wasn't at the stage where he could be haltered in the open, so I looped a catch rope over his head and led him into the crush. Once in there, he stood quietly while I slipped the halter over his head; he was often left unhaltered in the paddock and was used to this process by now. Once he was caught, I led him into an open area and began working with him; hoping that the holiday had been good for him, I held my hand out to say hello. Normally he would have tossed his head away to avoid contact, but today was different. Instead, he reached his head forward and bumped his forehead into my hand. Shocked at the human contact, he threw his head sideways and looked at me in surprise; then, working up his courage, he reached his head forward again. I brushed his head lightly with my hand and he shifted back nervously. For 15 minutes this continued. Each time, he would allow the contact for longer, until finally he stood still while I rubbed his head for more than a few seconds. It was the first time in almost six months that Elder had initiated human contact, and it was an overwhelming relief — he was now back to the stage he'd been at just a week out of the muster.

The next day Elder was even better, and the day after there was yet more improvement. It was the first time he had progressively improved over a period of three days, and I was hopeful that I'd finally made a breakthrough. However, the next day he stalemated, and it was another

TOP
Showtym Girl with
her foal, Impy.

BOTTOM
Promise's filly, Secret.

Top
Elder at the beach — his third time being handled after a couple of months' holiday with the mares.

Bottom
A few days later, Elder was sedated to be shod for the second time.

few weeks before I could safely stand beside Elder and touch him on the neck. The patience Elder was teaching me was amazing, as was how much my expectations had lowered — even the simplest improvement gave me the greatest pleasure and I enjoyed working with him each day to see the minute changes.

After a week of handling, the vet returned to sedate Elder and drop him to the ground so that we could re-shoe him. Although he had made some improvement, he was a long way from anyone being able to touch his legs, let alone pick them up, and, with his lameness worsening and his shoes getting looser by the day, it was important that we get them dealt with. Once the first injection was done, in the crush, I led Elder into the open yard. By now he was unstable on his feet, and sedated enough to have undergone most surgeries, but he needed to be on the ground for his hooves to be trimmed and shod. Walking quietly up to the heavily sedated horse, the vet laid a hand on his neck — and like a coiled spring Elder reared up and spun, lunging forward, his teeth passing just millimetres from the vet's face and dragging his glasses off his head.

It had happened so fast that I hadn't been able to stop him. Vicki and Amanda looked at me in shock, finally understanding what Elder was truly capable of. For the past couple of months they had often suggested that I put more pressure on him, to try to get better results, while I was happy with the minimal progress he was making. Every time I worked with him I felt he was just one wrong move away from snapping, and the only thing stopping him was a genuine trust for me — he seemed to understand and respect that the little things I asked of him were achievable.

CHAPTER 17

Viking takes on Europe

Amanda and Viking's last
evening before they flew overseas.

Amanda and Viking competing in their first 1.40–1.60-metre Grand Prix in 2012.

The showjumping season was now well under way but there was a noticeable hole in the team, with one of our best horses missing from the line-up most weekends. Amanda's favourite pony, Showtym Viking, was only competing at a handful of shows because she was finalising his sale into Europe. Since his glory days dominating in the Pony Grand Prix series, when he won many classes, including the National Pony Grand Prix and Pony of the Year titles — the two most prestigious pony events in the Southern Hemisphere — he'd gone on to have many successes up to 1.50 metres against larger horses and had also competed at Super League and World Cup level.

Viking was Amanda's horse of a lifetime. Although she'd been offered big money from international buyers years earlier, she'd never been tempted to part with him. But, in the winter of 2014, Equestrian Sports New Zealand (ESNZ) changed its series heights, abolishing the one-star series. Around the country, horses that specialised in the 1.40-metre heights were suddenly without a series class to compete in. Since Amanda was 22 she was also ineligible for the Young Rider series, and the only option was the 1.50-metre Grand Prix. Although Viking had previously won at that level, it was a huge ask to expect the littlest horse in the field to jump over fences higher than himself every weekend.

The rule change made her question what was in Viking's best interests: was it fair to campaign him over such challenging courses every week, or would it be best if he went to a younger rider so that he could compete against ponies once again? It was a difficult decision. The ESNZ rules meant that, once ponies had been upgraded to compete as horses, they could never be sold or competed as a pony again in New Zealand; Amanda knew she would have to sell Viking offshore. She could keep him as a hack, but would have to drop him down to open classes instead of series classes, and it seemed a waste for such a talented pony to compete in less prestigious classes for only a fraction of the prize money.

Amanda had no doubt that Viking was one of the best ponies in the world; certainly no others were currently competing successfully up to 1.50 metres. Ponies were only expected to jump a maximum of 1.35 metres in international championship classes. Although the decision was heartbreaking, Amanda decided to sell him because she wanted the very best for Viking, and none of us could doubt her reasoning. Viking would thrive with a smaller rider over smaller jumps on the Pony Grand Prix circuit — the smallest he had competed for years — and the European surfaces were also superior to the often substandard ground conditions found in New Zealand.

Another factor Amanda had to consider seriously was how her riding was affecting Viking. His job was much harder now because he often had to jump from wrong distances because Amanda's eye was no longer conditioned to pony strides. Viking had once been her main horse, but Cassanova had now stepped up to World Cup classes and he had a longer stride, as did her younger horses; she was struggling with the transition between the 14.2-hand pony and the horses at 16.3 hands. It was taking a lot of mental focus to adjust back to Viking's smaller stride, which had once been so familiar.

Once people heard that Viking was on the market, Amanda received interest from Italy, France, England, Germany and Denmark — from Grand Prix riders vying for a spot on their national team through to the 10-year-old daughter of a World Equestrian Games showjumper, he was highly sought after. It was overwhelming for Amanda to deal with, as each time a new person enquired she carefully vetted the potential home to see what type of lifestyle they could offer him.

For Amanda the type of home was more important than the money. Viking's life in New Zealand had more freedom and adventure than most horses experience in a lifetime, and it was crucial that he continue to experience both the challenge of high-level competition and the fun of being ridden simply for pleasure. Finally, she selected a family from Denmark who had three kids aged 14, 12 and 10, which would mean that he would be passed on between siblings and stay in the same family for years. More importantly, the family had access to both stables and paddocks, the kids genuinely loved their ponies, and, like us, they competed more for the love of the horses than the fame or fortune. Even more importantly, they rode their ponies bareback and at the beach every summer — Amanda was convinced that Viking would be happy with them.

Amanda and Viking at the airport, en route to Europe.

The next few weeks were hectic, organising vet checks, insurance, contracts and flights. Since Amanda had single-handedly found a buyer without the help of an agent, there were many stressful things to organise. The most daunting one was Viking's height; because he was maximum pony height, the sale agreement stated that he had to measure as a pony on arrival in Denmark or the sale would be void — all of the risk lay on Amanda, including the price of the pony's international flights. While she was confident that he would measure in at the required 148 centimetres there was still a chance, however slight, that he would be too big — if that happened, the financial implications were huge, since she'd had to borrow the $30,000 needed to fly him overseas. After poring over the pros and cons, she was adamant that she should go ahead; her gut feeling told her this was the best path for Viking's future, and we supported her wholeheartedly despite the very real risk that she would find herself on the other side of the world with an oversized pony and having lost vast sums of money.

On 10 December 2014, Amanda and Viking headed off on their journey. She was accompanying him to make sure he settled at his new home; since the family had purchased him sight unseen, she desperately wanted to meet the people with whom he would live out his days, and could only hope that they were as lovely as they had sounded on e-mail and telephone. After a three-hour truck drive and then another four hours waiting at the airport, Amanda loaded Viking onto a cargo plane and settled him into his narrow box beside an eventer. The crate was small, with no room for the horses to lie down during the 30-hour flight, and Amanda checked them often. Both horses quickly lost their appetite, and she spent much time hand-feeding them.

Just before the plane landed at Heathrow, the pilots invited her forward to the cockpit to watch the landing and she caught her first sight of England. Approaching the runway, she let out a sigh of relief: she and Viking had arrived safely on the other side of the world — until that moment, the furthest Amanda had ever been from home was Australia. After being unloaded from the plane, Viking was tired but still had to wait another two hours to be checked by a vet. Although he'd lost a bit of

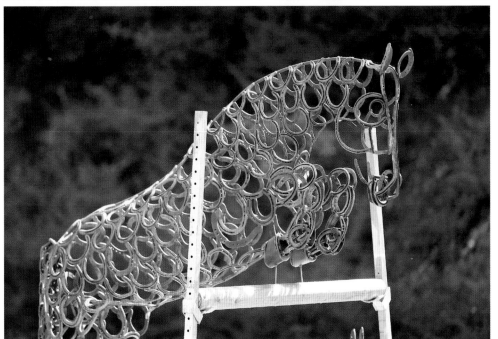

Top
Amanda and Viking placed second in the Young Rider of
the Year at the 2011 Horse of the Year show.

Bottom
A life-sized sculpture of Viking made by Dad for Amanda on her return from Europe.

weight, his general health was fine and he would pick up condition fast once he was settled at his new home. Ahead of him now was a two-hour drive to Kent, where he would be stabled for three days before being driven across Europe, eventually arriving in Denmark. Amanda wasn't joining him in Kent; the next morning she flew to Copenhagen to stay with Josie, a Danish rider who had been based at our stables two years before.

With four days to fill until Viking arrived, they visited stables, rode horses and went sightseeing. At the first stables Amanda saw, she instantly regretted her decision to sell Viking into Europe; the stalls were small, dark and dank, and the horses remained stabled for most of their lives — it wasn't the kind of life she wanted for Viking. Distressed, she called home and told us how depressed the horses had been — the only good thing was that they didn't know any other life and had nothing better to compare it with. Trying to calm her, we reminded her that she'd been happy with the sound of Viking's new home; she'd seen photos of the property he was going to and had asked all the right questions. She just needed to wait and meet the family rather than stressing out and imagining the worst.

After a good night's sleep Amanda was a little more optimistic, and distracted herself visiting castles and playing tourist with Josie. In their spare time they went to showjumping stables and Amanda found one yard with a number of exceptional young jumpers for sale. There were plenty of outstanding horses with so much scope that they put many of the New Zealand horses to shame — over fences their hindquarters appeared to be doing handstands and they cleared the jumps with plenty of room to spare. Amanda's awe quickly faded, however, when she heard that the horses had been trained with trip wires and wrapping to make them over-jump; a dangerous and illegal practice that compromises a horse's welfare and can cause them to flip and sustain serious structural damage. The practice results in an artificial representation of the horse's natural ability, and over time they lose some of their initial scope. The yard averaged one horse sold per day and it was obvious that it was a numbers game: whatever was necessary to ensure that the horses sold for premium prices.

Amanda and Showtym
Viking performing their
victory lap at the 7-Year-Old
Horse of the Year in 2011.

Wrapping, although not unheard of in New Zealand, is more common overseas. It is something we have never considered doing, or ever felt was needed. If horses are sound through the body, have natural talent and are ridden well, they will develop clean, scopey jumps anyway and, more importantly, they jump from the heart — because they enjoy it. There are so many horses that are drilled and disciplined into jumping; for these horses it becomes a job, something they do well not to please us, but to avoid punishment.

During the previous showjumping season, one of Vicki's fellow competitors had stood at the practice jump with his hand on the rails — a good way of telling which horses had been wrapped. Some changed their normal rhythm as they approached the fence and over-jumped, expecting the rail to be raised when they were in mid-air. Seeing what was happening, Vicki cantered in to jump the fence and, as she approached, glanced down at the man and told him she'd never wrapped a horse. Her horse, unlike those that had reacted, maintained its rhythm and jumped normally, unaware that a person standing beside a jump can have a negative connotation.

The night before Viking was due to arrive in Denmark, Amanda met his future owners and was immediately put at ease. They were some of the loveliest people she had ever encountered, and they all had fun attending an art exhibition of some of the world's best artists.

The next morning, they drove across the country to collect Viking so that he wouldn't have to detour and have another nine hours added to his truck drive. Amanda was excited to see him, and, considering how far he had travelled, he was in surprisingly good spirits — although he was more interested in eating than in the three young kids who had lined up to meet him for the very first time. When they saw him, they laughed in relief at his size; he was much smaller than they had expected. Several of their other ponies were taller when they lined him up next to them, and they had no doubt that he would measure as a pony.

After being turned out in the paddock and having a good feed, Viking was feeling his old self and they brought him in to ride. Amanda had already watched many videos of the three kids riding, but was even more impressed in real life. Viking loved his young riders and jumped around a small course while Amanda gave them a lesson — it was the only chance for her to see the kids riding him, because they were leaving on their Christmas holiday the following afternoon; Viking would have a well-deserved rest while they were away.

That night they took Viking to be measured and he walked in at 148 centimetres, easily the required height. The risk Amanda had taken in flying him to Europe had been worth the gamble, and she couldn't have been happier. He'd found a home with three beautiful young riders who would enjoy him to the full, and in just a few weeks he would begin competing on the prestigious European circuit. In the summer, along with their other ponies, they would be taking him to spend two weeks swimming in the ocean and being ridden bareback on the beach — it didn't get much better than that.

Amanda's last ride on Viking was bittersweet; she jumped on bareback and bridleless in the indoor arena, cantering around at liberty. As she gave him a final kiss she reminisced about old times; they had had so many adventures together over the past five years and he had made so many of her dreams come true. She hoped he would do the same for his new riders.

CHAPTER 18

Back in work

Amanda and Nikau's
first ride back
since Equidays.

TOP
Liberty foaling during one of our Showtym Adult Retreats.

BOTTOM
Independence was born with severe facial deformities and had to be euthanised just hours after birth.

— 204 —

For two months, Argo, Anzac, Nikau, Tullock, Battle and Trooper had rested in the paddocks on the hills, with very little human contact. It was great for them to relax in a herd situation and have the opportunity to unwind mentally; we had asked a lot of them over the past months, especially the Stallion Challenges horses. While the horses loved being in a herd again, however, it soon became obvious that they missed human attention. Every time we went to visit them they would canter up to the gate to say hello, and it was an awesome feeling. Even in such a large paddock, with several other horses, it was always the Kaimanawas that came up to us first, the showjumpers slowly making their way along at the back.

Anzac in particular missed his training, and after eight weeks of holiday he jumped out of the paddock and trotted up the driveway towards the stables. Too busy to find time for an extra horse, I returned him to his paddock; but the next day, he trotted down the drive again. Having well and truly got the point that he wanted to be home, I put him in the paddock beside the arena and began working him again. Vicki decided that the other Kaimanawas were ready to bring back into work too, so we led them down from the hill. Amanda wasn't due back from Europe until the New Year, so Nikau and Hoff would have another few weeks of holiday.

Elder and the mares were already in the home paddock, and we were waiting impatiently for Libby and Honor to give birth. Finally, in early December, during one of our Showtym Adult Retreats, one of the girls came running over to the arena to get us; Libby was on the ground, foaling. We rushed over to watch. It was the first time we'd seen a mare foal during daylight hours, and we were excited to watch the miracle of birth unfold. Although she hadn't been handled much in the past few months, Libby was totally relaxed about having an audience, and Vicki helped her while about 20 people watched from the fence line. Only minutes passed before the foal appeared, and we were captivated by the newborn's efforts to struggle out of the placenta. When it finally emerged we all froze, however; this long-awaited foal didn't look normal and there was a huge deformity on the filly's head.

Libby got to her feet and turned to nuzzle the foal; but, instead of licking it dry and encouraging it to stand, she turned and walked away to graze, uninterested. Confused, we stood to the side and waited for her to return, but over the next half an hour she never did. Catching the mare we led her back to the foal, but she turned her head away and ignored it; worried, Vicki stepped forward and rubbed it vigorously with a towel.

By this point we'd been on the phone to the vet a number of times, and after seeing photos he was convinced it was a dummy foal, a deformed animal incapable of surviving on its own. If the mare had been still in the wild, it would have been the herd's natural instinct to leave it behind to die. The vet would come out as soon as possible to look the foal over but he told us to prepare for the worst — there was a high chance that it would need to euthanised. He had seen similar cases, and the horses generally died from natural causes in the early years of life as the deformity enlarged, affecting the nasal passages, imploding the eyes and making it difficult for the horse to graze and breathe; if things were as bad as he feared, it would be far kinder to put the filly down now.

Keeping our hopes up, we hand-milked one of our other broodmares so that the foal would have something to drink. Slowly she gained strength. We got her standing, and once Libby saw the filly moving she returned to her side and stayed with her — as attentive as she should have been originally. Side by side they remained for the next few hours, but when the vet arrived and examined the foal it was obvious that putting her down was the only solution. You could see the deformities in her jaw, tooth and skull structure, which would only worsen with time. Libby stood close by when the foal was put down, and as the filly lay on the ground she came over to lick her and tried pushing her to stand. Realising that something was wrong, she stood guard over the filly's body, waiting by it during the night and the following day as well. At the vet's suggestion we gave Libby the time to grieve, and it wasn't until she walked away from the lifeless body that we entered the paddock and collected it, carrying it away to bury.

FOR THE NEXT FEW WEEKS WE SWAM and hacked the Kaimanawa boys over the farm, gradually bringing them back to full fitness. Libby joined them in the river — after losing her foal it was nice for her to have a distraction, and the cool water helped ease her swollen teats. It was a time for the horses to just enjoy life, and we didn't ask anything of them or teach them anything new — there is a time for learning and a time for fun, and we were focused on the latter.

With the showjumping season in full swing, we struggled to find the time to fit the Kaimanawas back into our routine; in comparison with other trainers in the competition, our horses probably had the lightest workload leading up to the finals at the Horse of the Year show. In the past the Kaimanawas had been our focus during the off-season, but with the Stallion Challenges we'd had to commit to working right through our busiest time of year. Summer became a frantically busy time for us; since we were so often away competing with the showjumpers we frequently had to play catch-up during the weekdays, fitting the Kaimanawas' training into any spare time we could find.

When there weren't any shows we were also busy with our Showtym Camps and Adult Retreats, and the Kaimanawas quickly learnt to play their part; although most riders are required to bring their own horses to camp, we do offer a few lease horses for riders flying in. It was a huge responsibility for the wild horses and we were always careful that we trusted them before trusting them with others.

Argo, with his quiet nature, was used for beginner riders. This suited him well, since he was too young to join in on jumping lessons. He particularly loved swimming in the river and the kids enjoyed doubling and tripling on him as they did laps in the water. Anzac was also reliable and fun for the kids, and quickly became a favourite. He especially excelled in the jumping lessons, although at the first few camps we only assigned him riders that we had trained ourselves; since it was so early in his training, we didn't want him getting confused by someone with a different style of riding.

It was an incredibly important part of the Kaimanawas' training to get used to other riders; not so much for Argo, who was big enough for Vicki to compete and keep long-term, but for Anzac, Nikau and many of the others, who would eventually have to have child riders since ponies can only be competed by riders under 17 years of age. Over the past three years we have saved 24 adult Kaimanawas from slaughter, and seven foals have been born to the mustered mares; realistically, we can't keep them all. Momento, Ranger and Remembrance were our favourites from the 2012 muster and they still graced our paddocks, and we were already sure that Argo and Elder would always have a home with us.

Since the muster, there have been many times when I've been disappointed that Anzac is so small, because if he were bigger I would keep him for myself. We considered the possibility of keeping some of the Kaimanawas from the 2014 muster for our Showtym Camps but, although it's a valuable experience for them for a season, it's not the life we want for them. The wild Kaimanawas have a remarkable ability to bond with one person, and they deserve to have someone make them the centre of their world.

Argo and Anzac were ridden by many riders during these summer months, and for Vicki and me it was incredibly rewarding to see how well-behaved they were. It was a while before I would part with Anzac, but I was already excited for him to be starting a new chapter in his life — he was going to make a fantastic kid's pony. But, for now, I was glad to have our time together and to know that the life experiences he was gaining at our property would set him up well for a long and happy future.

Tullock and Libby, although not ready for kids to ride yet, were also joining in on camp activities. They were ridden by Alexa and Georgia, a friend from the South Island who was based at our place to compete over the summer months. Every week the horses gained new skills, until they were also versatile and good for jumping and trekking in large groups, and reliable enough for a range of riders.

Trooper was also coming along nicely, with Kirsty making slow but steady progress. It had taken four months before he could be backed, first because of lameness and then because he'd been sidelined with a virus, but now he was well and truly making up for lost time. Every day they played in the river. Trooper loved to swim laps with the showjumpers — Kirsty even taught him to cope with her standing on his back, and he would walk and trot in the river with her like this; when she fell into the

Top
Anzac, Argo and Momento, our Kaimanawa mare from the 2012 muster, having fun in the river.

Bottom
Anzac and Olivia, one of our camp riders from the South Island,
during a jumping lesson at our Showtym Camp.

— 209 —

Trooper and Kirsty at the beach, three weeks after Trooper was ridden for the first time.

Bottom
After seven months of patient handling, Elder was comfortable being touched below the neck.

water beside him he would wait while she dragged herself back on, and then they would continue on their way.

With New Year fast approaching, Vicki brought Battle down off the hill and started handling him; he'd gone unsound again a week after Equidays, and since Vicki was still sore from her fall she had left him turned out longer than was ideal. Apart from her three showjumpers, Argo was the only other horse she was riding, but she was hesitant about bringing Battle back into work. He'd only had about 20 rides before Equidays and was still inexperienced; she didn't want to risk getting injured again, and she knew this was a distinct possibility since he hadn't been ridden for so long.

After a week of basic groundwork, Vicki got Alexa to hop on Battle in the water and swim him a few times; then, hoping for the best, she saddled him up and hopped on herself. He felt tense for the entire ride, and although he cantered around the farm willingly enough Vicki didn't see the need to continue with him in the competition. In the grand scheme of life, having Battle in the finals wasn't a priority; she decided that it was far better to look after her body and focus on her most important horses rather than risk injury on a green horse fresh out of the wild.

Vicki and Showtym Cadet
MVNZ winning the
Ultramox World Cup at the
Taupo Christmas Classic.

CHAPTER 19

On top of the world

With Amanda still overseas and Vicki only competing a handful of horses, we headed down to the Taupo Christmas Classic, one of our favourite events of the season, with just four horses — the fewest we had competed at a show in years. I competed Copycat for the last time and Vicki had her three 'big boys' with her and, although they hadn't competed for four weeks while Vicki recovered from her injuries, they were all looking and feeling good.

But the night before the show Premier, Vicki's most experienced horse, stepped on a pumice rock and bruised his sole. Although he wasn't lame, his foot was very tender, and Vicki scratched him from the warm-up classes so that he could rest and recover, hoping to nurse him along so that he would be okay to start in the World Cup on the final day of competition.

Levado was also another strong contender for the weekend and looked to be winning in the Welcome Stakes, jumping a fast, clear round. But just before the last fence in the jump-off, he stumbled. Managing to recover, he jumped the fence, but brushed the top rail and they finished on four faults, well out of contention. On landing, Vicki drew him back to a walk and patted him, but she could feel an unevenness in his gait, and once she was out of the ring she dismounted to look him over. He'd lost a shoe in the mud and torn part of the hoof wall off with it. Even once shod again he wasn't sound, and he too sat in the yards.

With two of her best horses sidelined, Vicki's focus turned to Cadet. While the youngest and least experienced of the team, he was one of her most promising horses, and over the next two days of competition he placed in both the 1.40-metre class and the Grand Prix; he had never felt better. Although it was Cadet's first show back since Vicki had fallen off him at Waikato, she was confident that he was on form and decided to start both Premier and him in the World Cup the following day.

That night at the auction, where the World Cup horses were 'auctioned off' for charity, she asked the show organisers to hold Premier from the bidding. Although he was sound and feeling good, he'd never competed at that level without a warm-up class and she wasn't confident he'd jump well. Cadet, who was relatively unproven at World Cup height, had a highest bid of just $100 — 80 per cent less than for the favourites. Everyone was unsure how he would jump after his scare at Waikato.

The following day both horses were presented for the Trot Up, their coats glistening with health, their manes beautifully plaited. The vet passed both as sound and fit to compete, and they returned to their yards to wait until the big class. While the horses were massaged and given some time to graze, Vicki went off in search of her sports psychologist to get her head in the game. They talked for over an hour about her plan for the class, her plans for the future and how she was going to achieve both.

A month before, Vicki and Premier had been named in the High Performance Accelerator Squad, made up of just a handful of riders that ESNZ was training to represent New Zealand in international team events, with the long-term goal of having horse-and-rider combinations suitable for selection for the Olympics and the World Equestrian Games. It was a huge honour to be invited, and something Vicki had not been eligible for previously due to a lack of horsepower. While she was one of the most successful Grand Prix riders in the country and had placed in many Super League competitions, she had only had a handful of starts at the elite World Cup level. She'd never been in a position to afford good horses; both Cadet and Premier had been written-off by others as difficult and dangerous, and she'd produced them herself. Now, as nine- and 11-year-olds, they were stepping into their own and were rated as some of the best horses in the country.

For Vicki to maintain her position in the Accelerator Squad, it was important for her to start getting consistent results at the top level. On Premier, she had placed in her only World Cup that season, and she was determined to improve. A clear in the opening round of a World Cup class was her most important and immediate goal. Winning could come later, but right now consistency and accuracy would ensure a solid foundation.

Over the past eight years Vicki had competed in a handful of World Cup classes, and, although she had often jumped clear in the second round, a clear in the first round had eluded her. It didn't help that her horses were young and inexperienced, but Vicki was confident that Cadet and Premier now had the experience to hold their own at the highest level, and she was excited to see how they would jump that afternoon. After walking the course, she returned to the truck and got the horses ready to compete, then mounted and rode down to the warm-up ring.

The class was soon under way. Vicki and Cadet were the first combination to start, and from the very first jump it was obvious that he was in his element. After heavy rain the ground conditions weren't ideal, but it didn't affect Cadet at all and he jumped effortlessly, confidently navigating the first half of the course. Approaching the triple, he jumped clean down the line of obstacles before powering around to the final two fences on the course — faultless. In his previous World Cup, Cadet had jumped clear until the tenth fence, when rider error had caused him to refuse. This time, Vicki made sure she gave him a careful ride, ensuring that he had the best approach to the oxer and the final planks, which were built to maximum height. He cleared both with plenty of room to spare. Her goal to jump clear had been met, and as she cantered through the finish flags Vicki leant forward and patted Cadet — he had proved that he was capable of jumping at the highest level, and Vicki was very proud of how far he'd come since she'd bought him two years earlier.

The next horse was eliminated at the fifth fence, and many other combinations dropped rails. So far, Cadet was the only horse to have jumped clear. It was now time for Vicki to return to the arena, hopeful that she could produce another faultless round on Premier. Even without a warm-up class he jumped well, dropping just one rail and ranking her in the top four riders going into the final round.

Eight combinations returned for the second round, jumping in opposite order of their faults. The jumps had been raised in height, and many of the horses faulted at the 1.60-metre fences. Premier started well, but after dropping a rail at the triple bar he got flustered and took out another one, dropping them to sixth place. With a pat, she rode from the ring — the mistakes had been rider errors and now, having been around the track once, she knew the spots to watch out for and was well prepared to correct them when she piloted Cadet around the course.

Settling into Cadet's saddle, Vicki returned to the practice arena, warming him up slowly. He felt fresh and powerful beneath her and she was quietly confident. She had been thrilled with their first round and, having already jumped clear, she was confident that they could do it again. The horse was obviously capable, and now it was up to her to get him to each fence with the best approach and just the right canter. The winner would be the rider with the least amount of collective faults from both rounds in the fastest time, but today Vicki wasn't concerned about winning. Instead, she was focused on another clear round.

Entering the ring, she trotted in front of the crowd and, when the bell rang, she asked Cadet to canter, approaching the flags. He cleared the first jump effortlessly, and she turned and approached the next fence at a concise angle. Jump after jump, he soared around the course, not touching a single fence and finishing with a good time, and — more importantly — zero faults over both rounds of jumping.

Only one combination now had to jump, also sitting on zero faults. Katie Laurie and Kiwi Iron Mark had been auctioned off for the most money the evening before, and were by far the most experienced in the competition. If they could jump clear and in a faster time, the win would be theirs. Vicki didn't wait around to watch them jump, instead focusing on her horse. Giving him a hug, she cooled him down slowly and his head stretched low in relaxation as he trotted. Her back, which had been causing problems, twinged and she loosened her back brace. In the ring, with all the adrenaline, it had been easy to forget her soreness but, now that the class was over, the pain had returned with full force.

As she circled the warm-up ring, she heard the announcer call her into the arena as the winner. Kiwi Iron Mark had dropped a rail in the final round, and to Vicki's surprise he had also completed the course in a slower time. During the prize-giving Vicki was unable to stop smiling. Winning the class was one of the biggest achievements of her life and she was immensely proud of Cadet — a double clear round, over such a difficult course and so early in his career, was a huge accomplishment and she was excited about what the future held for him.

Top
Vicki and Ngahiwi Showtym Premier finished sixth in the World Cup.

Bottom
Vicki and Cadet during the prize-giving for the Taupo World Cup.

CHAPTER 20

The festive season

Seven of our Kaimanawas from the 2014 muster join with our friends on a ride down Whananaki Beach.

Two young colts I photographed
at sunrise on the way home from
the Taupo Christmas Classic.

After the Taupo show we only had a few days before Christmas, and on the drive home I detoured to the Waiouru Military Training Base to photograph the wild Kaimanawa herds before heading home later that evening. I headed into the Ranges with an army guide at sunrise, and saw more than 150 wild horses that day — the most I had ever seen. The others went straight home with the showjumpers, putting them out to rest and recover from the strenuous weekend.

We all spent the following day unpacking the truck, reorganising the gear and tidying up the house for Christmas, as we had family coming to stay. We worked quickly, since we were keen to head up north for a ride at Mitimiti in search of the feral horses that run wild in the sand dunes there.

Unlike the Kaimanawas, the horses at Mitimiti are privately owned by local Maori. One local guy, having read *For the Love of Horses*, got in touch and offered us two free horses in exchange for starting a third under saddle for him. Having been promised the ride of a lifetime when we went up to collect them, we headed north with Argo in the truck — the rest of us would ride horses already up there. We'd ridden at Mitimiti a number of times; it's one of our favourite places to ride and this time was no exception. The trekking horses we had were well trained and a few even ambled, an artificial gait the local Maori often train their horses to do because it offers a smoother ride. It was a first for us; we'd always wondered what it felt like.

As we rode along Mitimiti Beach we found several feral horses grazing near the dunes and, finally, we came to a large paddock where two young stallions had been herded for us. We now had a challenge ahead of us — catching two horses, which had never been touched or haltered, in an open area and then loading them onto the horse truck. Argo proved to be very useful and, once the stallions were rounded into yards, the real challenge began. Since both were too wild to approach, Vicki cornered and then haltered them from Argo's back. Neither stallion appreciated being caught and they lunged at Vicki several times — but Argo always put him in his place. Having been a wild stallion himself, he wasn't intimidated by the other stallions, whereas many domesticated horses would have been.

Once both horses were haltered, the easiest one was taught to lead and Alexa led him 3 kilometres down the beach to the truck, with Vicki on Argo, dragging the feistier stallion behind. Getting them loaded on the truck proved to be a daunting task, as at the base of the ramp the stallions reared and refused to approach. After 15 minutes the first stallion walked up the ramp, but the second was more difficult, so we led Argo up to give the stallion confidence. Eventually the stallion followed. On our way home we stopped to admire a stunning horse by the side of the road. He was an impressive stallion, one of the most beautiful we had seen. His owners had named him Osama Bin Laden, after the terrorist, because he often eluded capture and jumped out of his paddock. Despite his reputation, he was their favourite and they weren't interested in selling him; but they offered us his son, Saad Bin Laden, for $500. This six-year-old stallion was also strikingly beautiful and appeared very sweet. We were told he was good under saddle, although we didn't have time to ride him. Feeling that he was underpriced, we gave them $800 and loaded him onto our truck with the others.

Once home, however, we realised that we'd made a mistake, and quickly regretted the impromptu purchase. Like his sire, Saad was an escape artist. The first day we had him, he scrambled up a vertical cliff to scale the 2-metre-high post-and-rail fence at the top, before jumping another fence to join the mares. He soon settled, though, and turned into a promising young horse.

With Christmas now upon us we enjoyed a lie-in, the horses waiting somewhat impatiently to be fed. Up until a few years ago we had been caught up in the commercial hype and big spending of Christmas, but four years earlier we had made the decision to boycott the festivities completely, taking our miniature horse and our dogs to the local retirement home and spending the day talking with the elderly and hanging out with a lovely group of strangers who enjoyed being visited at a time when they are so often forgotten.

Since then we had developed a more relaxed and enjoyable Christmas Day tradition with family and friends. We spend time playing our favourite games — Scum, Greed, Risk and Bat Down — with much friendly rivalry between us. Lukas, our builder and friend, had given us a hand-carved set of wooden pieces called Viking Chess, and we spent a lot of time in the paddock throwing batons at the chess pieces — our accuracy leaving a lot to be desired. In the afternoon we saddled our favourite horses for a ride (it's safe to say that the three new stallions weren't among our selection), and challenged each other in jumping competitions, including childhood favourites like Take Your Own Line and Tip 'n' Out. Perhaps the reason these games are so enjoyable is our complete lack of competitiveness; although we love the thrill of winning in the competition arena, at home we are simply out to have a good time and are willing to give anything a try. It's more about social time with the important people in our lives than the need to win — there is nothing worse than an overly competitive person taking the enjoyment out of a friendly competition.

On Boxing Day we loaded some horses onto the truck and headed out to the beach for three days of camping. We had seven of our Kaimanawas from the latest muster with us, and also Rover, one of the new feral stallions. Vicki had spent some time with him and he could be led and touched on the head and neck — in just 48 hours he was more advanced than Elder and Hoff were after seven months of domestication.

As soon as we arrived at the beach, we jumped on some of the horses bareback, heading down to the estuary to swim them. The water in the channel was completely out of the horses' depth, and because the Kaimanawas had never swum there before they were hesitant, unsure where they would find dry land; they kept circling back to shore. Jumping off, we swam in front of them and, trusting us, they followed closely behind. Once their feet touched down on the far side, they relaxed, and happily swam back and forth across the channel.

Once the horses were safely put away we headed down to the beach for a swim on our own, and later that evening we played hopscotch and Four Square. It was fun to reminisce over the games of our childhood, although we argued, half-heartedly, about the rules; since none of us could remember them properly, we made up our own versions. One of the international riders who was based at our stables to compete for the season, Kat, kept quitting, not willing to play a game she wasn't good at. She was so caught up in how she looked that she wasn't looking around to see that we were all equally as bad — the only difference was that we were having a good time failing and were more than willing to laugh at our own expense when things didn't go as planned.

With a little encouragement Kat joined in on the games, and eventually enjoyed herself like we'd known she would. Interestingly, she had exactly the same attitude when riding and we had to continuously encourage her to step out of her comfort zone. Our first mission this trip was to get Kat swimming a horse, so I offered her the chance to ride Anzac in the water. Although she'd been riding for years, swimming a horse wasn't something she'd done before and she refused to even try, worried that it would go wrong. It took quite a lot of cajoling before Kat finally hopped on Anzac and followed us out into the water — a huge smile on her face. Without our persistent and tireless determination, this life experience would have been one she'd missed out on; in hindsight Kat was happy she'd tried it, and the next day she was the first to catch her horse, excited to swim again.

During Kat's nine months with us we got her to try many things for the first time, and it was a positive and rewarding experience for her. We aren't the type of people who look down on someone for failing; instead, we celebrate them being willing to try — surely this is the very first step to success. From a young age we have learnt that the best memories are made when we challenge ourselves to try new things; we couldn't think of anything more boring than sitting on the sidelines and watching the world pass us by.

The next two days dawned with clear blue skies and we spent time relaxing and swimming the ponies at high tide. At dawn, when the beach was quiet, we rode the horses around the point and cantered along the ocean beach. It was a good opportunity for the horses to have some fun, and a great environment for Trooper's very first canter. Elder and Rover joined in on the adventures, following closely behind on the lead; by the end of our beach holiday, Vicki was riding Rover in the estuary with the other horses.

We returned home in time to celebrate New Year, spending the day

Top
Crossing the estuary on the Kaimanawas.

Bottom
Even though he was only three days out of the wild, Rover was
so relaxed he lay down in the estuary for a roll.

TOP
Vicki and Rover getting to know
each other in the shallow waters.

BOTTOM
Elder and I enjoying the beach.

hanging out with friends. In the evening we decided to make a time capsule, and made a list of fun and silly questions to answer. On the other side of the paper we wrote our five-year plans and also our highlights from 2014. It was a great opportunity to reflect on the things we had achieved, silly moments that had made us smile, and our proudest accomplishments. Sometimes it's easy for time to slip by without celebrating the good moments or learning from the bad, and for everyone it was an inspirational and rewarding task, giving us a new focus for the upcoming year.

We were so caught up in the moment that it took a while to notice that Kat had gone quiet. Looking over, I watched as she struggled to come up with things to write on her highlights list. So far all she had written was *graduate from college* and *come to New Zealand*. I asked her what was wrong, and she said that she felt so bad about herself — we had a long list of things and she could barely come up with a handful.

Showing her my list, I pointed out some of the things I'd written down — such as riding horses in the snow, playing Viking Chess, a new favourite food I'd discovered, a four-year-old boy asking in all seriousness whether I'd marry him, as well as the more obvious things like winning People's Choice and Runner-Up Wildlife Photographer at the New Zealand Geographic Photographer of the Year awards. I'd named my list the *Smile Highlights of 2014*. I told her to write down anything and everything that had made her smile over the past year. Soon her page was filled with personal bests and adventures she had enjoyed: black-water rafting, skiing, playing cowgirl at the Wild West town, placing in her first 1.05-metre showjumping class, seeing Kaimanawas in the wild, flying a glider plane and swinging on a trapeze were just some of the things she'd done during her time with us. So many of the things on her growing list were things she'd been terrified to do at the time, but in hindsight they were the things she was proudest of. It made her realise that the things she'd done outside her comfort zone had left her with the best memories. This revelation made her more determined and excited to try new things, and make the most of her remaining time in New Zealand.

Once our lists were completed we sealed the answers in a bottle and buried it, promising to have a reunion in five years to laugh over the answers and reminisce over old times. Just before midnight, along with friends, we caught our favourite showjumpers — even the World Cup horses were included — and took them for a ride around the hills in the dark to welcome in the New Year. When we returned, just after midnight, we decided to seize the moment, and after the horses had been tucked into bed for the night we ran to the lake to swim in the pitch-black darkness.

The holiday season was topped off with 'wing walking' strapped on the roof of a Tiger Moth plane, and we were all excited to try it — even Amanda joined us although she'd only just arrived back in the country. Standing on the roof of a plane while it flies 1000 metres above the ground might seem like a crazy idea, but we loved every minute of it; like our horses, we get bored if things become routine and we're always willing to try something new. Over the years we have discovered that an adventurous nature can be learnt and bravery gained — jumping out of aeroplanes and off cliffs, and white-water rafting through grade-five rapids, didn't come naturally to any of us. For Amanda and me especially, heights began as a fear we wanted to conquer; we hated being limited by this so set about overcoming it. Five years ago I made a list of *100 Things to Do*, and the many adventures we've had since then most assuredly wouldn't have happened if we didn't actively seek out opportunities to try new things.

It's amazing what putting pen to paper can accomplish — we're huge believers in writing down our goals, dreaming big and making the most of every opportunity. All of us live only once; we are committed to making the most of each day, each week and each year because we don't want to look back later in life and regret the chances we didn't take.

Vicki, Amanda and I, along with eight friends, went wing walking
on a Tiger Moth plane to celebrate the New Year.

CHAPTER 21

Bareback jumping

Vicki and Showtym Levado GNZ dressed as pirates during the novelty Speed Special, where they elected to compete bareback.
Ned Dawson

TOP
Anzac and I jumping
bareback and bridleless.

MIDDLE
Argo and Vicki (under
cover) practising for
the obstacle class at the
Stallion Challenges final.

BOTTOM
Amanda and Nikau
training at home.

E arly in the New Year we were e-mailed the list of requirements for the final leg of the Kaimanawa competition, the Stallion Makeover at the Horse of the Year show. There were three qualifying classes. The first was a horsemanship class where the horses had to perform a set workout, and when we saw the level of training required we were initially shocked. It seemed like an extreme amount to train a wild horse, and we questioned how much time we were willing to spend schooling. To a certain degree, we would rather receive a score of zero for some of the compulsory moves than have to train our Kaimanawas extensively — our horses' welfare always comes first and we value the fun rides as much as, if not more than, the days we spend training.

Obviously we weren't the only ones with concerns about the level of training required for our once-wild horses, and a week later the committee sent out a revised plan. The new workout still had plenty of challenges but was much more manageable. Ready to see just how much the horses were receptive to, we switched our minds into training mode and, for the first time since Equidays, began teaching our horses new things.

The first of the required moves was to side-pass over a 4-metre pole, and within minutes the horses had grasped the basic concept — not perfectly, by any means, but they had a vague idea of what we were asking and were eager to please. We had forgotten just how fast the Kaimanawas learnt new things, and over the next week we continued to make good progress — in five days, with no more than a hour of arena work behind them, all three of our Kaimanawas had reached the minimum requirements for Horse of the Year.

The second class was an obstacle course with nine elements. The horses would be required to go over, under, around and onto a range of unfamiliar objects, and we felt sure this would be a fun and interesting class. Wanting to prepare the horses for anything and everything they might encounter, we constructed random obstacles around the property; and no matter what was asked of them, they always tried.

The last qualifying class was the freestyle, and this was what we were most excited about — a chance to showcase our horses as individuals and share their unique talents with the public. Argo had a number of skills up his sleeve, Anzac was jumping and working well bareback and bridleless — and Amanda kept telling us that she had the best idea, but she just hadn't thought of it yet. With time running out we suggested that she start coming up with a plan, but each time she'd smile cheekily and remind us that she'd beaten us both at Equidays, with exactly the same relaxed, leave-it-till-the-last-minute approach.

From these three qualifying classes, only the eight Kaimanawas with the highest combined scores would be eligible for the Stallion Makeover final; we knew we needed to start investing serious time into the horses. Although there were no required moves in the final, the horses did have to complete a timed obstacle course and there was a large freestyle component to give us the opportunity to show off what they'd learnt. We had only eight weeks left to train and we'd already lost valuable time — unlike us, most of the other trainers had been working their horses consistently since Equidays.

THE FOLLOWING WEEKEND, ANZAC AND ARGO were loaded onto the truck alongside our showjumpers for the World Cup Finals. It was the first event they had attended since Equidays; we'd been invited to do a performance to open the prestigious event. Vicki and Argo had been working on a new move, which they were hoping to incorporate into their freestyle in the Stallion Makeover, and I was glad for the opportunity to get Anzac used to crowds again.

The World Cup Finals are hosted in one of the most picturesque arenas, with a beautifully presented but equally daunting ring. Even some of the experienced competition horses were worried about the statues, plants and sponsored jumps that were scattered around the ring, and for wild horses it was overwhelming. On the Friday and Saturday we were given the opportunity to ride the horses in the arena so they would become accustomed to it, and within minutes Argo was calm and relaxed; nothing much fazed that horse. Anzac was initially worried, but quickly settled and did everything he was told — he was noticeably more relaxed than at Equidays, and I hoped that the exposure would prepare him mentally for Horse of the Year.

That afternoon Anzac competed in showjumping classes, with Makaila aboard since I was too old to compete a pony. It was the first time he had competed in a traditional competition and I was like a proud mother watching him work for the younger rider. There is something incredibly rewarding in knowing that you have taught a horse everything it knows, and as I watched him warm up I felt like I'd achieved what I'd set out to do: I'd taken a stallion from the wild, then tamed, befriended and trained him into a happy and responsive mount. Anyone watching from the sidelines would be hard-pressed to guess his background and, although inexperienced, there was no doubt that he was just as capable as the other horses in the class.

The next morning, just moments before the World Cup began, Vicki and I rode our Kaimanawas into the ring to entertain the spectators. Argo was the first to go, and without any gear to guide him he performed a flawless demonstration. Halting in the middle of the ring, Vicki jumped off to get him ready for the second part of her performance and I began my bareback and bridleless work with Anzac.

Like Equidays, the atmosphere was buzzing and Anzac was distracted. He'd warmed up beautifully out the back, but now he was missing half my cues, rather unsettled by everything around him. Things went from bad to worse when he cantered around a corner and spooked at a life-sized rhino sculpture that had been hidden from view; while I struggled to keep my balance and regain control, he bolted towards Argo, slowing only when he was close to the other horse. Once he was reassured that the rhino wasn't in pursuit he returned to his workout, jumping over an upright, and bowing before finishing. Standing quietly at the entrance, I then watched as Vicki stood on Argo's back while he cantered around the arena and jumped, a flag billowing behind them. The things that she could do with that horse were impressive.

The Kaimanawas were soon returned to their yards and the World Cup jumpers brought out to compete. Vicki was riding Cadet and Premier, and Amanda was on Cassanova. The horses jumped well, with Vicki getting fourth place and Amanda finishing fifth. Although Levado wasn't in the biggest class, he was still the star of the show. Over the weekend he won the Speed Championship, the Grand Prix Super Series and the Speed Special, which had been a novelty class for the public to enjoy. Each of the riders had been required to compete in costume, racing against the clock to jump around a 1.20-metre course in the fastest time. Vicki had forgotten to bring a costume to the event, so pieced together a pirate's outfit out of paint, cardboard and clothing. She had two horses competing, and on the first one she jumped well but only received a score of four for her costume, style and difficulty. Other riders were receiving scores of nine as well as clocking up significantly faster times, and Vicki was left wondering how she could top things off to receive the highest combined score — she had nothing else to add to her costume and it was obvious that the judges would score that low again, so she decided to increase her level of difficulty and remove Levado's saddle.

Vicki had often jumped bareback over the years, but this would be her first time attempting to win a speed class, with its sharp angles and even tighter turns. When she entered the arena there was a gasp from the crowd; although Levado was one of the best speed horses in the country he wasn't the easiest to ride, and everyone leant forward to watch. There was a tough time to beat, but from the first fence it was obvious that Vicki was riding to win. As we watched anxiously from the sidelines, we prayed that she'd stay on — it would be so easy to fall off the horse if he turned too tightly or got the wrong distance going into a jump. As they cleared the last fence there was a sigh of relief from those watching, followed by huge applause when the judges held up their scores — Vicki had received a 10, and had also jumped around the course in the fastest time.

Not long afterwards Vicki competed bareback again, this time in the Speed Slalom at Tauranga, raising $1000 for the CatWalk Spinal Cord Injury Trust. Like at Taupo the horses had been 'auctioned off' for charity, and someone had doubled the winning bid provided that Vicki rode bareback. Always up for a challenge, Vicki stripped Levado's saddle and entered the ring as her first competitor lined up at the start. The starter's hand dropped and the riders urged their horses forward, galloping around the course, with Vicki the clear winner. She returned to the arena four times, and each time managed to stay just ahead of her

Vicki and Showtym Levado GNZ
received a score of 10 from all
three judges of the Speed Special.
Ned Dawson

opponents, who were all competing in saddles, and she eventually won the final match-off.

Back at home I was in a bit of a dilemma. Unlike Vicki's impressive jumping displays with no saddle, I wasn't sure I could pull off my freestyle on Anzac bareback and bridleless like I'd planned. Although I trusted him completely and he worked perfectly at home, the World Cup Finals had made me question whether he would cope with the atmosphere at Horse of the Year. To place well he needed to be soft, relaxed and totally accurate in his workouts; and if the environment stressed him, like I feared it would, I would be better to use a saddle and bridle.

Since I had no other tricks up my sleeve, I started experimenting with new ideas to wow the judges and began training Anzac to stand on the flat deck of a friend's ute. Vehicles had been his main fear since the muster, so this worked well, increasing his confidence and teaching him something impressive at the same time. To prepare him I led him on and off a few times; then, vaulting onto his back, I jumped him up onto the ute before turning on the forehand (where the horse's front feet remain still while the back feet complete a circle around them) and jumping off again. Quite pleased with Anzac, I dismounted and gave him a handful of feed as a reward.

Sure that I had the beginnings of a great idea, I checked the rules of the competition and was disappointed to learn that only Land Rovers were allowed in the Premier Arena where the freestyle event was to be held; since they didn't make anything with a flat deck, it seemed like my training had gone to waste. I began working Anzac with just a rope around his neck again, hoping that enough practice would stand us in good stead. Every day he got better and better, until my control and steerage rivalled the work I could do in a bridle and I was quietly confident.

Amanda had also come to realise that time was running out, and began thinking up ideas for Nikau's freestyle. Up until now he'd only had about a third of the mileage of Anzac and Argo, but he was very special in his own right and Amanda was excited to showcase his strengths . . . she just had to figure out what they were. Over the next few weeks she began riding him bareback, experimenting with a range of tricks and jumping

him over small obstacles again. He was very willing and receptive —
learning new things wasn't his problem; rather, it was Amanda finding
the time to consolidate the lessons he was learning.

CHAPTER 22

far North adventure

The Kaimanawas join us on one of our Showtym Far Northern Adventures.

Top
Riding the horses on Ninety Mile Beach.

Bottom
A wild colt watches us in the Aupouri forest.

In early February we found ourselves with a free weekend and decided to organise a spontaneous Far North adventure. Several times each year we take clients and friends up north for two days of intensive riding in search of the wild Aupouri horses, and we always have the time of our lives. Unlike the Kaimanawas, which are genetically unique and isolated, the Aupouri horses are a feral population rather than a truly wild one — this is because the Aupouri locals have been known to release old or injured horses into the herds.

Almost 1000 horses roam the northern-most part of New Zealand — three times as many as in the Kaimanawas — but because offshore companies own the forest where they live the Department of Conservation doesn't muster the horses and they are left free to roam. The Aupouri horses are a similar colour, size and type to the Kaimanawas, although in the past they were far more diverse in appearance. Many years ago, coloured horses roamed the Northern regions, but despite all the times we have ridden through the area we have never seen a pinto, dilute or appaloosa — most have been rounded up, and now only solid-coloured horses remain. If coloured foals are born on the odd occasion, the locals are rumoured to capture them at a young age since they are the most sought after.

On the first day we parked the horse trucks at Ninety Mile Beach and everyone saddled up for a ride — there were 14 horses altogether. For an hour they rode down the beach; then, since we had special permits, they cut through into the forest in search of wild horses. While the others rode, Mum and I had a swim in the ocean then drove down the forestry roads to look for Aupouri herds. Within minutes we found three bachelor stallions, and then in quick succession saw herd after herd in the felled region. At the top of No. 3 road we saw 13 horses spread out below us, and parked the car to watch them. They were too far away to photograph and, hoping I wouldn't scare them, I slid down the steep embankment and quietly approached, only moving a few metres at a time before waiting and letting them get used to my presence.

When I was about 20 metres away, three of the yearlings broke off from the herd and approached curiously. I froze, and when they paused I slowly sank to the ground to make myself less intimidating. With renewed courage they started towards me again, the rest of the herd turning to watch. Slowly the bay filly in the front crept closer and, feeling bold, the two greys soon followed. Behind them four foals trotted over to investigate and, now worried, the mares soon joined them. Twelve wild horses stood there, nearly surrounding me, and off to the side I could see the stallion watching me closely, unsure whether I was a threat.

Remaining still, I held my breath as the horses pressed in closer; soon they were too close to fit in the viewfinder of my camera. Placing it quietly down beside me, I turned my attention to observing the horses. Again, the curious bay filly stepped forward until she was standing just a metre away from me. Realising that there was no danger, the others stepped forward too, and soon I was encircled. Out of the corner of my eye I saw the stallion approaching. As I had nowhere to go I remained still, watching as he drew closer; eventually he stood just a few metres away, his head peeking over one of the mare's backs as he looked down at me.

Minutes passed, but still I held the horses' interest. I was worried about moving in case they became frightened, but looking up the hill I was reassured to see Mum still standing there, watching. Since the horses weren't going anywhere I inched backwards, hoping to make a quiet retreat. Beneath me a branch snapped, and the sudden noise caused the horses to scatter in fright. Making the most of the opportunity I turned and headed up the hill; behind me the yearlings circled back and followed me. When I reached the car they paused, then turned and cantered back to the safety of the herd.

Mum and I ventured further into the heart of the forest, and soon came across two stallions fighting under the shadow of the pines. It was a breathtaking sight as the last of the evening light filtered through the trees behind them, and we watched as the bay stallion admitted defeat and spun, galloping into the forest, his herd following closely behind.

By the time we returned to the main forestry road, our group of riders was in sight. On either side of them, herds scattered, trying to put distance between themselves and the mounted horses. Five of the Kaimanawas from the latest muster were on the ride; Argo, Tullock, Nikau, Trooper and Libby walked with a spring in their steps, watching the wild horses with interest.

A herd of Aupouri
horses watches us from
under the pine trees.

Driving ahead we waited for them at the truck, and as they rounded the final corner I did a double-take — Vicki was riding Argo backwards.

Everyone was animated, telling how close they had got to one of the wild herds; as they described the horses, we realised that it was the same ones that had surrounded me. While everyone else was unsaddling, Vicki and Kirsty rode Argo and Trooper down to the beach. I followed closely to watch as Vicki first walked, then trotted and even cantered facing backwards, her balance perilous. Occasionally she had to place a hand on Argo's rump so that she stayed on, but the young horse never faltered, ears forward as he bounded down the beach. Trooper followed behind him with Kirsty taking both hands off the reins and spreading them wide, 'flying' as they circled around and cantered back towards me.

Trey, a young boy who'd been learning to ride with us, ran down the beach to join me — he'd taken Libby out on the ride, and had quickly unsaddled her and left her tied to the truck so that he could see Argo working. Together we stood watching as Vicki removed Argo's bridle and rode him with no gear. By now they were a polished act, and with just Vicki's voice to guide him he halted and then lay down on command. Running over, Trey climbed on in front of Vicki and sat steady as she put Argo through his paces again. It was the first time Argo had doubled, but he barely noticed the extra weight and, although Vicki had no bridle or rope to guide him, he was attuned to the subtle shifts of her body for direction and listened closely to her voice for speed.

The next day we drove half an hour south, to the top of the Ahipara hills, and headed out on a ride through the petrified kauri gum fields, then across kilometres of sand dunes before reaching the beach on the west coast. This is one of the most diverse and picturesque locations in New Zealand, and in particular the windswept sand formations never cease to amaze us. Part of the appeal of a Far North adventure is that we never ride the same route twice, and this time we explored the most southern route, precariously riding along the edge of the sand dunes before sliding down a steep track through dense scrub to the river below.

Urging the horses forward we cantered through the river, droplets cascading around us as we powered towards the ocean. In front of us,

Vicki cantering Argo backwards
along Ninety Mile Beach.

Lukas's horse shied and he went flying into the water. Behind him, Libby jumped sideways to avoid a pile-up and Trey also fell off, landing knee-deep in the water but still holding the reins. Around them everyone halted, doubled over with laughter. On closer investigation we realised that the massive bulk that had scared the horses was not a log at all, but a dead humpback whale. It had been there a long time and had lost most of its form.

Soon we were on our way again, galloping down the length of the beach, enjoying the sun and the surf as we began the long ride home. Bringing the horses back to a walk, we threaded our way around each bay while the west coast surf pounded against the sand. Again, Vicki turned around and rode Argo backwards, chatting to everyone as we rode along. A haphazard collection of baches lined the shore of each bay, the only access being a drive along the beach at low tide. Distracted by our surroundings, we almost missed the herd of wild horses standing poised on the rugged cliffs behind, but they had obviously spotted us and the stallion gathered up his herd and moved them away, cantering down onto the beach and powering through the sand and surf until they were out of sight. Continuing on, we trotted around a bend and watched as the herd spooked at an oncoming vehicle barrelling down the beach; spinning, they turned back the way they had come and we rode up the sand dunes to let them past. We don't often see the wild horses on the beach, and seldom such a large herd, and we watched in silence as the 16 horses passed us in single file.

The rest of the ride passed quickly and we jumped rocks and driftwood as we made our way back to the truck. Argo was exceptionally honest; although he hadn't jumped much, due to his young age, Vicki often took him over natural obstacles. After the Stallion Challenges he would join her competition team, and she was looking forward to competing him in the 4-Year-Old series the following season. Eventually the truck came into sight, and we quickly unsaddled and rode the horses into the crashing surf to cool them off before loading them up for the two-hour drive home.

Top
A herd of wild horses on the cliffs, just moments before they cantered down to the beach.

Bottom
Cooling our horses down in the ocean after a four-hour ride through the petrified
kauri gum fields, Aupouri sand dunes and along Ninety Mile Beach.

CHAPTER 23

Natural instinct

Hoff on neighbouring farmland, after he escaped through fences and over a river. He tried to attack Amanda multiple times when she caught him and led him home.

Top
Every time someone passed within metres of his paddock, Hoff
would pin his ears back and charge at the fence.

Bottom
The three diseased molars that were removed from Hoff's mouth helped
ease much of his pain, but did nothing to improve his personality.

In the six weeks since Amanda had returned from Europe she had worked tirelessly with Hoff, hoping that after more time off to recover in the paddock his disposition would have improved. Going up to the hill where he grazed with other horses, she entered the paddock, naïvely hoping that his basic instinct to attack would have lessened. When he saw her, however, he eyed her up and charged, galloping at her with ears pinned back and teeth bared. She was too far away from a fence to get to safety, so grabbed a fallen branch from the ground and raised it above her head, swinging it around and around like a gladiator; it wasn't until he was just metres away from her that he swerved, before circling back for a second attempt. Continuing to swing the branch, Amanda slowly stepped backwards until she was able to dart under the fence to safety.

As she stood there, shaking, the angry horse continued to circle, galloping at the fence to try to intimidate her again and again. Amanda did eventually get him caught, catching him from the other side of the fence. Once the rope was on, he calmed a little and she was able to get him back to the stables, although she kept him on a very long rope and always kept fences or trees between her and the angry horse as a precaution.

Not once since Hoff had arrived at our property had we ever felt he was truly happy with life. Amanda was often reduced to tears, not wanting to work with a pony that obviously disliked both humans and domesticated life in general. She wasn't willing to give up on him, however, and spent hours with him in the hope that she could win both his trust and his affection. Twice she actually felt as though she'd made a breakthrough, and both times she called us outside to show us how well-behaved he was. Expecting a huge improvement to justify Amanda's level of enthusiasm, we had followed her outside — and quickly realised that her expectations of Hoff were even lower than we'd thought. She was excited simply because she could lead him and touch him on the head without a fence separating her, and because on both those days he only threatened to bite her occasionally.

Hoff's good behaviour never lasted for long, and without warning he would quickly revert to his more dangerous persona. In early January, eight months after the muster, Hoff tried to attack Amanda three times in less than 20 minutes; although she'd come to expect this by now, he had never been quite this bad. Hoping that something had been overlooked, we had the vet, eye specialist, skeletal therapist and dentist check him over again, but his previous issues had long been resolved and there was nothing to explain his behaviour. If there had been a chance that his aggression was pain-related we would have done everything possible to work through it.

As Amanda released him into his paddock, images from the past eight months flashed through her head like a movie; there hadn't been a single time she'd worked with him when he hadn't tried to hurt her, and she no longer had any hope of winning him over. He wasn't even suited to be retired as a paddock mate, because you would never be able to enter his paddock safely; and with a sick feeling she began to seriously entertain the idea of putting him down. She came over to discuss her reasoning with us, and both Vicki and I supported her decision; if she didn't make the call now she would have to live with the guilt when he finally hurt someone, and then have to put him down anyway.

Distraught, and feeling like she'd failed the horse, she called KHH and requested permission to have him euthanised. They gave it; there had been plenty of forewarning and, although disappointing for everyone, they understood where we were coming from. We had always believed that every horse was tameable if trained correctly, so for us the decision about Hoff was particularly hard. When do you quit on a horse's life? With DOC it had been an easier decision: his quality of life was severely compromised and it was for his welfare that we had decided to say goodbye. But with Hoff the decision entered a grey area; ultimately we would be euthanising him for our own welfare as much as, if not more than, his.

By now we had worked with more than 30 wild horses, including 17 adult stallions, and Hoff was the only one we had never trusted. While we have had accidents with some and been intimidated by many, never had we felt that any of the other wild horses meant us bodily harm with such serious and ongoing intent. Many horses become difficult and dangerous from bad handling and worsen over time, but Hoff had been difficult right from those very first moments in the stockyards, and over time he had neither worsened nor improved. Either he had been born rogue, or he had developed a brain injury from the trauma to his head, which had turned him aggressive.

With Hoff's end date rapidly approaching, Amanda was struggling with her feelings; she had never had to make a decision like this before and it was causing her to question everything. Had she done *everything* in her power to give this horse a second chance at life? Would giving up on him now be something she would live to regret? With less than 10 hours to go to the final day she rang up and cancelled; there must surely be something she hadn't tried and she felt as though she needed to exhaust all possibilities before giving up.

Over the next month, Hoff still failed to make progress, and every day he was just as dangerous as always. If we passed his paddock to go and catch other horses, he would gallop along the fence line trying to get at us. Then, to make matters worse, he learnt to escape from his paddock; when Amanda went out the back to catch Nikau one day, she heard the pounding of hooves behind her and caught sight of a black blur just metres away. Hoff shouldn't have been in that area, and luckily Amanda was close enough to the fence to be able to scramble to safety.

Shaking, she came inside and fixed another date to have Hoff put down; but again she couldn't commit to giving up on him, cancelling once more in the final hour. Amanda booked in and then cancelled Hoff's demise three times in total, but in the end her hand was forced: Hoff escaped from his paddock and twice chased people at the neighbouring swimming hole. We had to face the reality. Even if we managed to break through to Hoff, which at this point seemed unlikely, how many years of perfect behaviour would it take before we could ever trust him in someone else's hands? We feared that if he was ever frightened or hurt he would revert to his instinctive defence mechanisms, and we weren't willing to take the risk, with either our own lives or those of others.

HOFF REMINDED US OF A TEENAGED BOY we'd been working with earlier that year; he'd had a messed-up childhood that had left him with major anger issues, and he was also gang-affiliated. Hoping that she could make a difference in his life, Vicki took both him and his younger cousin under her wing and taught them to ride; something they had a natural affinity for.

Every day they came down to ride the horses, and within weeks they were confidently cantering over the farm. Vicki's rules were simple: while they were on our property they weren't allowed to smoke, swear or drink, they had to help look after the horses and they had to respect us. They quickly learnt that there would be no second chances, and when they were around us they were polite and courteous — they understood that if they wanted the privilege of riding they had to clean up their act.

The improvement in their behaviour both at home and at school was significant. Since we didn't have a horse really suitable for the older boy, Vicki bought him a lovely, kind mare and leased it to him on two conditions: the first that he had to take over all responsibility for her and the second that he stay out of trouble — there should be no reason for the cops to have to visit him. For several months he continued to improve, and then slowly he started falling by the wayside and nothing we did could get him back. After all the time we'd poured into him, it was disappointing to see him slip back into his old lifestyle; but we hoped, at the very least, that we had shown him enough good to offer him a glimmer of hope for the future.

The younger boy, who was just 10, spent every spare second with the horses, and with time his passion and commitment grew. He'd been suspended from school countless times, was adept at stealing and was often caught smoking, drinking or taking drugs, and neither his mum nor his teachers knew how to handle him. But we didn't see a naughty kid; we saw a troubled boy who was desperate for a purpose — and from the first time he sat on a horse, he had a new focus in life.

He quickly came to look up to all of us, and in his eyes Vicki could do no wrong. When she was shoeing the horses he would ask to hold the hoof, and every time he had a riding lesson he asked questions, keen to learn as much as possible. Just three months after he had sat on a horse for the very first time, he rode one of our camp ponies at his first show,

Top
Elder grazing with his lead mare Honor and their foal Valor, who was born at our property in late February.

Bottom
Although Elder found most people intolerable and preferred not to be touched, he was never dangerous or aggressive without provocation. Unlike Hoff, we always felt safe entering Elder's paddock and could turn our backs on him without fear of being attacked. Although it took months of patient handling, I could safely touch him on his head and neck while he remained relaxed and content.

and they jumped around the 90-centimetre class with just one dropped rail. From then on he dreamed of being a farrier or a showjumper — and then, after galloping a horse for the very first time, he thought that being a jockey might be a good option, too.

Although this lad lived a couple of hours away, he spent all his holidays with us. Sometimes, if life got too overwhelming during the school term, he would give Vicki a call; no matter what the hour or the inconvenience, Vicki would hop in the car and go to pick him up, and he would cling to her like a lifeline. Having someone that he could rely on was massively important, and after the long drive back to our home he would run inside and hug each of us before heading outside to ride. We always loved having him to stay, and had quickly came to love him like a little brother.

Hoff was too like the older boy. Despite us giving him every opportunity, he still chose the wrong path and there was only so much we could do to help him. To a degree, Hoff needed to meet us halfway; regardless of how much pain he had been in or the trials he'd faced in the past, we could only lay the foundations for a better future. Like the younger boy, he had needed — and been unable — to step up and take the decision to make the most of what life offered him.

CHAPTER 24

The final countdown

In the months leading up to Horse of the Year, Dad spent hours working on a life-sized sculpture of a rearing Kaimanawa stallion, which was to be gifted to the winner of the Stallion Makeover of the Year at the finals.

In the final weeks leading up to the Horse of the Year show we were constantly busy, and the Kaimanawas were only one of the many things on our long list of what needed to be done. The deadline for my second book was fast approaching; it was due to the publisher only days after the Stallion Makeover. Vicki was riding full-time and prepping a team of six jumpers for the Horse of the Year, as well as schooling and competing clients' horses, and was also overseeing the finishing touches to her new stable complex. Amanda was busy too, struggling to catch up on life after her time in Europe and, more recently, a week in Sydney competing the horse she'd sold into Australia during the winter.

On top of all of this we were filming part-time for the television series — catch-up interviews for a full day once a week right through until after the competition — and we were also trying to finalise plans to go to America in April. We had been invited to compete in the Extreme Mustang Makeover, one of the largest wild-horse events in the world, and were keen to raise awareness about the plight of wild horses on an international scale. The logistics of trying to organise this was a whole new playing field for us, with many hours going into planning such an extensive trip; we were flying out just two weeks after Horse of the Year and would be based in America for 100 days to tame the Mustangs.

With so much to do and so little time, there were moments when we wished we didn't have the added pressure of the Stallion Challenges; but we were also thankful. The requirements for the challenges motivated us and, in the middle of a busy competition season, made the Kaimanawas a priority — something they might not have been otherwise.

It is very rewarding to save horses from the wild, especially fully grown stallions, and there is also nothing quite like exceeding your own training expectations. For Amanda it had been a slightly more trying process, but Vicki and I could honestly say that we had never trained a horse to the level we had achieved with Argo and Anzac. This wasn't in a way that most people would understand — they certainly didn't jump higher than other horses we owned or perform flawless dressage moves, but the bond we had formed with them was impossible to describe with mere words. We were the sole reason that these horses were alive and it was very special knowing that everything they had learnt was because of the love and time we had invested in them.

The hundreds of hours we spent with our horses meant that we knew all their little quirks and their personalities better than anyone else, and we were able to sense what was normal behaviour for them and what was not. Just a month out from Horse of the Year, my once quiet and dependable Anzac changed; overnight he became spooky and naughty, and since this was so out of character I stripped the saddle off him and checked him over to see if he was sore. There was nothing obvious, but although he was working well I still had a feeling that something was wrong.

A few days later we headed south for the Waitemata Super League show, with Anzac and Trooper joining us. On the Saturday both of the Kaimanawas competed in Show Hunter, and although the pirate-themed arena scared Anzac he jumped around kindly for our friend and student Claudia. Trooper, who had only been under saddle for eight weeks, was hesitant yet willing; Kirsty jumped him in the warm-up classes.

The next day Kirsty, Mum and I took one of the trucks south to compete at the National Kaimanawa Show, while Vicki and Amanda stayed behind to compete in the Super League where they placed second and fourth on Premier and Cassanova respectively. At the National Kaimanawa Show the ponies arrived relaxed, but when they saw horses working in harness in the adjoining ring both of them were terrified. Although Trooper settled, Anzac never truly relaxed and both placed poorly in the in-hand classes.

We soon returned for the ridden classes. Trooper worked kindly on the flat, winning and placing in every class and finishing as Reserve Champion on the Flat and as Champion Hunter. Anzac was also more relaxed now that the harness horses were out of sight; although still not his normal self, he managed to win Best Pony Club Mount and three of his jumping classes, and finished as Reserve Champion Hunter behind Trooper. Although Anzac was jumping well, his behaviour at the show was atrocious, and seriously concerning. Never in my life had I ridden such a poorly behaved horse at a competition. Still convinced that something was wrong, I checked him over again. Finding nothing sore, I started treating him with a range of supplements, including some for stomach ulcers and grass-affected conditions. Within days he transformed; it was an absolute relief to have my quiet and sweet pony back — the difference really was that significant and immediate.

It's not the first time we have been confused as to why our horses have suddenly changed in behaviour, but these days we recognise the symptoms and are able to correct things sooner. Any changes in behaviour, either ridden or under saddle, are a reaction to something — horses don't go from being quiet and reliable to spooky, tense, difficult and stressed overnight for no good reason. Sometimes these symptoms are due to pain, but grass can also cause similar reactions, especially during the change of season or when moving horses to new properties. The worst case I'd seen was after I'd moved to Auckland with my showjumping mare a few years earlier. Within months she'd become unrideable; the experts weren't able to diagnose what was wrong with her, but she was constantly stressed and couldn't walk up or down even the slightest incline without bucking. After four months of expensive vet bills I was in absolute despair; my horse had gone from quiet and reliable to too dangerous to even mount, and I was almost at the point where I was ready to retire her as a broodmare.

As a last resort I sent hair samples away for testing — and this revealed that she'd been exposed to toxic levels of pesticides; the growth rings on her hooves also indicated the stress she'd been under since moving to the new property. That week we trucked her back north to home, and the change in grass was all she needed; within weeks she was her normal self, cantering over the hills on the buckle and soon competing again.

In the lead-up to Horse of the Year, Amanda was also having issues with Nikau, and many times she was left frustrated. Because of his setbacks, as well as her time overseas, he'd had fewer than 50 rides since the muster and Amanda wasn't confident that he was ready for the Stallion Makeover. She had hoped to focus on jumping for Nikau's freestyle, but he hadn't had time to develop this properly. He wasn't the bravest of ponies, and although honest he would often hesitate on take-off before snapping his knees up in beautiful form — there was no doubt he had the talent, but he lacked experience and heart. His schooling on the flat was coming along nicely, but Amanda got no enjoyment from working him on the arena — she felt as though he preferred to be out on the farm, or in the river, and so she only did enough to teach him the minimum requirements for the challenge. She saw no point in drilling her inexperienced horse simply to improve her chances of placing in the qualifying classes, and constantly reminded us that, regardless of how Nikau went in the Stallion Makeover, she was already a winner.

She had set out to save a Kaimanawa from slaughter and then produce him into a happy and willing horse that enjoyed life — and she'd achieved that. Nikau was a delight to take out on the farm and to the beach, loved swimming, had learnt a number of tricks and was well adjusted and interested in life. He might not be the best trained for the upcoming competition, but she was happy with the progress he had made — Nikau didn't need to be a show pony or a jumper in time for the finals, and she certainly wasn't going to compromise her training methods to rush him along. All of that would naturally develop over time.

Meanwhile, Argo was consistent and kept getting better and better, although Vicki had to be very careful about how long she worked him. Because of his baby brain, he only coped with about 20 minutes of learning at a time — any longer, and he would quit and say no. Because of this, most of his work was fun-based and very rarely did Vicki consolidate his lessons on the arena; instead she gave him many days off to rest, and when she worked him she was careful to keep his work enjoyable so he was fresh and interested. She still practised riding backwards and standing on him, and had also taught him to rear on command. Our favourite thing to watch, though — and the thing Vicki was most proud of — was their work with no gear. It was incredibly moving to watch Argo going through his paces, finely tuned to the slightest cue from Vicki.

Two weeks before Horse of the Year, Vicki's stable complex was completed and we held a stable-warming to celebrate. A year before, she'd bought 25 acres bordering the family farm and had then put in a huge 470-square-metre stable complex. Each of the 14 stalls was larger than most — it was the realisation of a dream for Vicki to have custom-made

TOP
Vicki standing up on Argo with no bridle to guide him. By
now Argo was well trained to voice command.

BOTTOM
Vicki practising jumping while standing in the saddle.

— 269 —

Top
Argo was lame and on box rest for the 10 days leading up to the Stallion Challenges finals.

Bottom
Trooper and Anzac at the National Kaimanawa Show, where they won
Champion Hunter and Reserve Champion Hunter respectively.

stables specially designed so the horses had maximum space and social interaction while they were indoors in wet weather and on cold winter nights. Once friends and family were assembled, she caught Argo and got him ready for a demonstration to showcase what he had learnt in the months since the muster. The absolute trust and respect they had in each other was inspiring, and no one had any doubt that he would be a tough act to beat in the finals.

As Murphy's law would have it, just days later Argo cut through the sole of his hoof and went lame — so severely that he stood holding his hoof off the ground and had to be kept in the stables on box rest. Day after day Vicki checked him over and treated his hooves to avoid infection, but as time passed with no sign of improvement she seriously doubted that Argo would be sound in time to compete. A week later he was still lame; but we were out of time — the showgrounds were 12 hours away in Hawke's Bay, and we needed to allow two days to travel and then additional time for the horses to recover at the venue before the first classes began. Vicki decided to take Argo anyway, and loaded him onto the truck alongside her showjumpers — although he wasn't sound yet, he had four days before his first class started and she hoped that he would recover in time. Amanda and I loaded our horses onto a second truck and so our road trip to Horse of the Year began; between us we had 11 horses competing, and it was going to be a busy week.

CHAPTER 25

Horse of the Year

Vicki and Showtym Cadet MVNZ
competing in the Silver Fern
Stakes at Horse of the Year.

TOP
Anzac and me during the Trot
Up for the Stallion Challenges.

BOTTOM
Anzac and me, Argo and
Vicki, and Nikau and Amanda
at Horse of the Year.

Amanda and I arrived at the Horse of the Year showgrounds late on Sunday morning, and we unloaded our horses and took them for a walk to stretch their legs. Vicki was a few hours behind as one of her truck tyres had blown just outside Taupo. Events like Horse of the Year are a massive operation, with lots of people needed behind the scenes to get the horses prepared and to the rings for the riders to compete. We had three horse trucks with us, complete with living quarters, and we camped out at the showgrounds for eight days. Besides the three of us, we had Kirsty, Alexa, Georgia, Lukas, Sarah, our parents and Miriam, our German groom.

A storm was brewing and, with Cyclone Pam due to hit the Hastings region hard, the storm preparations were well under way. Heavy rain and gale-force winds were expected overnight, and the show committee was under huge pressure to keep everyone safe. The 750 square metres of marquees were tied down securely, the first day of competition was cancelled and anyone arriving from after 3 pm on the Sunday afternoon through to midday on Monday, was being directed to the racecourse. With 2600 horses entered it was the biggest equestrian event in the Southern Hemisphere, and the committee wanted numbers kept as low as possible during the worst of the weather to ensure that every horse on the grounds was under shelter. Since most of our supplies were in Vicki's truck, we were enormously relieved to see her pull into the gates with just minutes to spare. Although the sky was grey there was no sign of rain yet, and as we unloaded the horses and settled them in their covered yards there were only the seagulls that had come inland to hint at the storm raging offshore.

On Monday we woke to rain, and although it remained with us for most of the day it wasn't as bad as had been expected. Thankfully, the eye of the storm had passed us by. We spent the day cleaning gear and, not wanting to brave the wet weather, I rode Anzac up and down the aisle of the covered yards to stretch his legs. The following day dawned sunny and clear. Although it was muddy, the high winds quickly dried the ground out, and as an extra precaution a helicopter was brought in after the wind died down to fully dry out the Premier Arena; with six days of jumping coming up, they didn't want the surface ruined on the first day. Soon the showjumping classes were under way; Vicki started off in winning form, taking out the 1.30-metre class on Levado.

Later that evening Argo was led from his yard, and for the first time in 10 days didn't walk out lame, much to Vicki's relief. Saddling him up, she took him to the warm-up arena to work but he was tense and distracted. She quietly worked him through the required moves for the horsemanship class and also her routine for the freestyle, but after 20 minutes gave him a pat and put him away. He wasn't listening, and nothing they had practised at home over the past few months was going to be possible if he was so fresh. His three-year-old brain was too busy with other things to concentrate, and Vicki knew that there was no point in working him longer. Hopefully he would be more settled by the next day; and, if not, there was nothing she could do about it — at least he was sound enough to compete, which was more than she'd thought possible only days before.

The next morning we groomed the Kaimanawas to perfection and led them to the far side of the showgrounds for the Trot Up. Since KHH is a welfare trust, they are committed to ensuring that every horse is healthy and sound, and it was obvious how much time the trainers had put into getting their horses in optimum condition. A few had been unsound and underweight at Equidays, but all 12 competing at Horse of the Year (of the original 19 in the Stallion Challenges) were now looking superb and were all passed by the vet as suitable to compete.

That evening the Kaimanawas were due for their first class, and we saddled them and led them to the arena. They had been due to start at five o'clock, but the showjumping class was running behind schedule and it was almost 6.30 before Nikau entered the arena, the first to compete. He started well; we watched from the sidelines as he worked through the required pattern, soft and relaxed — the best he'd ever been. Like at Equidays, he obviously knew when to step up his game. Approaching the trotting poles, however, Nikau hesitated and then jumped them rather than placing a hoof between each pole, losing valuable marks; he then cantered on the wrong lead before kicking out in the gallop. Apart from those three errors, though, Nikau had worked far better than Amanda had expected, and she leant forward and gave him a pat as she rode out of the ring, smiling.

Next up was Anzac. I had decided to do the workout with no bridle, a decision I quickly came to regret. Although I had 100 per cent steerage and control at home, and he'd been perfect in the warm-up ring just moments before, once Anzac was in the arena he forgot everything he'd been taught. The people and the trade stands that surrounded the arena were overwhelming for him, and it took everything I had to get Anzac to complete the required movements.

The last of our horses to perform was Argo. Although he wasn't as relaxed as normal, he was significantly improved from the day before and worked kindly, side-passing, changing between paces softly and completing the canter circles with a flawless flying canter change as he changed direction — the only horse to do so.

By the time the placings were announced and the winners had remounted their horses and re-entered the arena for the prize-giving, it was dark. Argo had held his own, placing fifth, but neither Anzac nor Nikau were in the final line-up. After Anzac's atrocious workout I had expected to be unplaced, but Amanda was blind-sided — although Nikau had obviously lost marks in the trotting poles and the gallop, the rest had been soft and kind and she was surprised that he hadn't finished in the placings.

The next day was spent showjumping. Vicki won another two classes and placed in several others; 2015 was shaping up to be another promising Horse of the Year for her. Amanda and Cassanova had also started strongly; although unplaced, they had competed well in the Norwood Gold Cup and the Lady Rider, the two biggest events of the show so far. Cassanova was now resting ahead of the most prestigious class on the Sunday. Amanda had high hopes of doing well in the richest and most prestigious class on New Zealand's showjumping circuit, the Olympic Cup. As inspiration, she had cut photos out of equestrian magazines to make a collage showing her dressed in the winner's red jacket, complete with Cassanova sporting the title rug, sash and garland. Amanda is a very goal-oriented person, and fully believed that visualising herself in the winner's circle would increase her focus and help her to achieve her dreams. In her room at home she had inspirational quotes scattered over her walls, her favourite being: *Shoot for the moon. Even if you miss, you will land among the stars.* She also had lists of goals printed out, both long- and short-term.

THAT EVENING THE KAIMANAWAS RETURNED TO COMPETE in the Obstacle class. There were nine obstacles in total and for each there were 10 points on offer: five for completing it, regardless of whether the horse was ridden or led, and five for how well the horse did. Each horse-and-rider combination had seven minutes to complete the course, which the riders walked beforehand. The first rider managed to work through only four of the elements. The second combination was Tina Fagan and Rock Star and they powered around the course, finishing well inside the time. Again the next few riders struggled, two of them falling off at the second obstacle, which was an imposing set of stairs that the horses had to climb.

Anzac and I were next. Our game plan was simple: try to get through all the obstacles in the required time, and if he hesitated at any I would dismount and lead him — it was better to get a couple of points less for a single element than miss obstacles completely by running out of time. Since the arena didn't back onto any trade stands, Anzac was much more relaxed. He strode confidently under the first obstacle and bravely walked up to look at the stairs, but he spooked and rushed backwards after placing a hoof on them. Worried about wasting time I quickly dismounted and gave him a pat to relax him; once he was focused again, I led him safely over the stairs. Remounting on the other side we continued on our way, completing all the obstacles with just seconds to spare. The time was so tight that if you hesitated anywhere you were at risk of not completing the course.

Next out was Argo. Vicki had obviously been observing the other riders, working out the best way of getting through the course. Everyone else had walked, but Vicki trotted through many of the obstacles, saving

TOP
Anzac circling Dad's sculpture during the Throughbred Floats Obstacle Class.

MIDDLE
Amanda and Nikau during the Saddlery Warehouse Horsemanship Class.

BOTTOM
Vicki and Argo safely navigating the stairs during their winning performance in the Throughbred Floats Obstacle Class.

Top
Vicki and Argo with the sponsors at the Obstacle Class prize-giving.

Bottom
Amanda and Showtym Cassanova competing in the Lady Rider.

valuable seconds. Argo gallantly attempted the stairs, climbing until his front legs were on the top, but when Vicki asked him to walk forward and lift his back legs onto the steps he shook his head in confusion. We had only trained him to stand on things and then back off — never to walk over objects. Vicki sat patiently urging him forward. He finally understood what she was asking and bravely stepped up and over, crossing safely to the other side — he was only the second horse so far to complete this obstacle mounted.

They quickly made up lost time, trotting over the orange carpet; and Argo gained maximum points for using his legs to push a Hoofball into the goal — many of the other combinations, me included, had halted the horses and used our hands to shoot, but Argo was a pro. He went on to complete the rest of the obstacles with ease, and Vicki gave him a pat before dismounting and rushing off to compete Levado in another class.

Nikau was the last to go and, like Argo, walking over the stairs confused him; he also expected to have to back off, but eventually walked over it ridden — now only three riders had completed this without either falling off or dismounting and Amanda's face lit up into a grin as she patted him. Working quickly to make up lost time, they moved efficiently through the remaining obstacles, but at the last — loading onto the horse float — he only got his front feet on before the bell sounded, losing a possible 10 points.

Vicki returned after having won the class on Levado, and was surprised when Argo was announced as the winner, with Anzac sixth and Nikau seventh. It was a huge achievement for a three-year-old to take out the Obstacle title and Vicki was very proud — right from their first ride together, Argo had put his trust in her and had bravely gone wherever she had asked. It had paid off in the ring; since no one had known what obstacles they would encounter in the class, it had been impossible to practise and was therefore a true test of each horse's nature.

The horses were returned to their yards, and I set to work clipping Argo's coat for the freestyle. Vicki was dressing as an All Black rugby player and wanted a silver fern on Argo's rump. Once he was done we all headed to bed; a film crew was arriving at six in the morning and was following us around for the whole day for a *Behind the Scenes* episode on Country TV — it was going to be a long day with the finals not finishing until 10 pm that night.

We were up at five to prepare the horses, struggling in the darkness. Under torchlight we groomed, painted and saddled the horses, and by 7 am we were at the ring, warming up; we couldn't believe how many people had braved the cold to watch the Kaimanawas compete at dawn. Again Anzac was the first of our horses to compete. Although he was capable of producing a workout to rival the best horses, I also knew that there was a high chance he would freeze in the ring; it was his first time competing in the Premier Arena and it was by far the most daunting; on every side trade stands surrounded the ring, and sponsor flags and signage decorated the sidelines.

As in his previous classes, Anzac warmed up perfectly and I was optimistic as he trotted into the arena. Within seconds, though, it was obvious that he was distracted by everything around him and all my hopes went out the window. Changing my routine, I worked with what he gave me; although he jumped and did some work without a bridle, it was decidedly less than what we had practised. I was past caring, however; like Amanda had said in the lead-up to Horse of the Year, we were already winners. Regardless of how Anzac performed in front of an audience, I was incredibly proud of my pony and knew what he was truly capable of. Of course it was disappointing that I couldn't showcase him to his full abilities in front of the public or the judges, but I didn't need their affirmation to feel like a winner. My horse was alive and happy, and over the past nine months we had achieved more than I had ever dreamed possible.

Next out was Argo, and although he worked well and gave a polished performance he was a little tense and Vicki performed a very basic workout compared with what he was capable of. She'd planned to ride him backwards and have him lie down, rear on command and work at liberty but decided to play it safe, not asking anything complicated of him. His placings so far had already guaranteed him a spot in the finals and she decided to save the impressive stuff for the Stallion Makeover title later that night.

Last out was Amanda, and we all lined the fence to watch. Very rarely had we seen her practising for this class and we were interested to see what she'd managed to pull together. Nikau followed closely behind Amanda as she rolled a trampoline into the arena and we watched in amusement as she did what she was best at: entertaining the crowd. After a failed attempt to vault onto Nikau, which was all part of the act, she brought the trampoline over and the pony stood calmly while she bounced beside him, then onto him and over him, showing just how tolerant he was. Next she stood up on his saddle and did a handstand off his rump, before bouncing from the trampoline over his rump to land in the saddle. She gathered her reins and continued to walk, trot, canter, jump and side-pass, and finished with Nikau pawing the air on command. She exited the arena to a huge round of applause and gave Nikau a hug. Of all of our horses, Argo may have performed the best but it was Nikau who had impressed us the most — Amanda was very pleased with what they had accomplished.

The placings were soon announced, and even with his simplified routine Argo finished sixth overall; Nikau placed seventh. Neither Amanda nor I qualified for the finals, but at that point we were relieved. Nikau had already exceeded Amanda's expectations and Anzac didn't need the added pressure of thousands of spectators. All our hopes now lay with Argo, and we were confident that he had a chance of taking out the title.

Vicki riding Argo one-handed in the
Stallion Makeover of the Year final, just
moments after dislocating her shoulder.

CHAPTER 26

*The Stallion
Makeover final*

The rest of the day passed quickly — between Vicki competing and the camera following us around, there wasn't much spare time. In between classes Vicki adapted her workout; after much thought she had decided not to ask Argo to lie down at the conclusion of his performance. On sand or sawdust his lie-down was automatic but on grass he took anywhere between 10 seconds and 10 minutes — it wouldn't look good if the bell sounded again before he had had time to complete the movement, like at Equidays. Deciding that she needed something else to wow the crowd with — as if riding backwards, standing up and working with no gear wasn't enough — she left us to brainstorm and hopped on another horse to compete.

Argo would literally go anywhere and do anything for Vicki, but the workout she currently had didn't showcase that side of his nature. We went for a walk around the showgrounds looking for inspiration, and within minutes found just what we were looking for. Parked at the go-kart area was a flat-deck trailer and I knew Vicki could get Argo to stand on it, do a turn on the forehand and then walk off. The owner of the go-karts quickly embraced the idea and offered to let us use it, and because only Land Rovers were allowed in the Premier Arena we then sprinted off in search of the reps — who were more than happy to lend us their Land Rover for the evening. Now all we needed was for Vicki to train Argo; she had just three hours before they were due in the ring.

Vicki returned shortly afterwards with two ribbons tied around her horse's neck: two of the clients' horses she was competing had placed well in the 1.25-metre Championship. When we explained our idea, she grinned and agreed to give it a go; catching Argo, she jumped on and we headed over to the go-kart area to see if he would be as obliging as we all thought he might. As we'd hoped, he walked straight onto the trailer, halted, turned and walked off. Wanting more of a challenge, Vicki nodded to Lukas, who was sitting behind the wheel of the towing Land Rover, and asked him to drive off slowly. Walking Argo forward, she followed closely behind the trailer and asked him to step up onto the trailer deck while it was still moving. Willingly he raised his forelegs and continued to walk on his hind legs to keep up with the forward momentum until

Vicki squeezed again to ask him to step up fully onto the trailer while it continued to move. Grinning, Vicki called out for Lukas to stop and turned Argo and jumped off. With a huge pat she reached forward and offered him a handful of feed, then led him back to the stables. Argo had a new trick, and although they'd only practised it for 10 minutes Vicki was confident that he would pull it off during the final; she could allow 30 seconds for this at the conclusion of the workout instead of getting him to lie down.

For THE NEXT TWO HOURS Argo wasn't Vicki's main focus any more. Before she rode in the Stallion Makeover final, she had two horses competing in the Silver Fern Stakes, the second most prestigious showjumping class of the weekend. Cadet and Premier had done well in their warm-up class and Vicki was optimistic — it was their last class before the Olympic Cup on the Sunday, and she was sure that both horses would be just as competitive as any of the other horses in the field. Finding a quiet place, she sat down for 15 minutes to prepare herself mentally. Right now, Cadet and Premier were all that mattered and she focused on the upcoming class, all thoughts of the Stallion Challenges put aside; Argo's time would come.

At six o'clock she mounted Cadet. She warmed him up well and when it was her turn she cantered smartly into the ring. The sun was setting behind the grandstand and harsh shadows were being thrown by the jumps, but Vicki wasn't worried — over the first four fences Cadet felt bold and powerful beneath her. Turning, they powered around to the fifth and on approach Vicki felt Cadet hesitate. Tightening her legs, she urged him forward but at the last second he stopped; caught off-guard, Vicki was thrown over his neck, hitting the wall hard before crumpling to the ground.

Standing on the sidelines we shook our heads, knowing how disappointed she would be, and waited for her to stand . . . but she didn't. It wasn't until they called for an ambulance that I felt the first shiver of worry, and I jumped the fence and ran across the arena with Mum and Amanda. Vicki *always* got straight back on her feet, whatever the injury — this was the first time ever that she'd stayed on the ground.

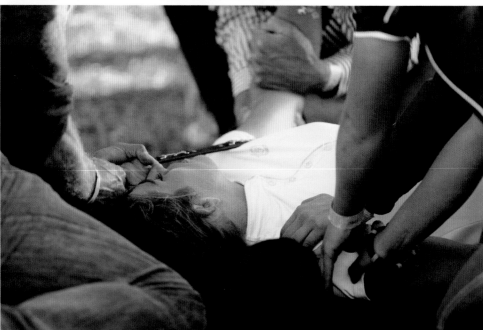

When we reached her she was lying still, her face deathly white. Beside her, a doctor was poking and prodding, trying to gauge the seriousness of the injury. Vicki was adamant that it was a dislocated shoulder and he quickly agreed. Knowing that time was crucial, they went to work trying to get the joint back into place. Agony was written all over Vicki's face; someone forced a whip into her mouth so that she could bite down on it to keep from screaming. Amanda and I both had to turn away, unable to see her in so much pain. No amount of manoeuvring was helping, however, and it was decided to get her to hospital to set the shoulder. We gently helped her to her feet and she walked slowly to the St John's buggy, gingerly holding her arm. The cheers from the crowd were deafening; after waiting with bated breath for the past 10 minutes they were relieved to see her moving.

Once she was backstage, Vicki was laid down on the ground and the doctor went to work again while they waited for an ambulance, three people holding her down. When she was offered pain-killers she shook her head; she didn't want anything that would affect her ability to ride, as, if they managed to get her shoulder back in place, she had every intention of riding Argo in the finals. Once assured that the medication wouldn't affect her ability to compete, however, she took some to ease the excruciating pain.

It was now seven o'clock and around us the Kaimanawas were starting to gather: the Stallion Makeover final was due to begin in just 15 minutes. I called the KHH rep to let them know that Vicki would have to forfeit; by default she would receive eighth place. Admitting defeat, the doctor said they would need to work on the shoulder under sedation at the hospital and helped Vicki to the ambulance, which had now arrived. Just before they drove off Vicki looked up in determination and demanded that the doctor try just once more. Unable to refuse, he settled her back on the ground, put his foot into her armpit and pulled while two other people held her down; and this time the shoulder popped back into its socket. Although still in agony, she thanked the doctor and told him he was amazing; the worst of it was now behind her.

Since no one was able to convince Vicki that riding wasn't worth the pain, we called KHH and told them that she planned to ride after all — then we ran back to the yards to prepare Argo. The first horse was already in the ring, competing, and Argo was due in the arena in less than 25 minutes. While Vicki had her shoulder strapped beside the ring, the girls uncovered, groomed and saddled Argo, and I set to work painting his silver fern. We got him to the ring with only minutes to spare, and Vicki made her way slowly over to the horse. Taking the reins, she laid her hands on Argo's head and told him to look after her, then slowly mounted, being careful not to bump her arm. Quietly she warmed up and it quickly became obvious that she was unable to use her left hand at all; but beneath her Argo was relaxed and settled, completely unconcerned by the thousands of people looking on, or by being ridden in the dark under spotlights. He was 100 per cent focused on her, and Vicki shook her head in disappointment: this was Argo at his absolute best and she had no doubt that he would have pulled off a magnificent workout if she'd had two hands to guide him.

With such a recent injury, and in so much pain that she was struggling to perform even the most basic of movements, Vicki's planned routine was impossible. With no time to prepare anything else, and really not capable of pulling off many of the moves she'd trained the horse to do, she rode into the arena. At this point there was no chance of her winning, but she would do what little she could. She knew that many of those in the audience had come to the show to see Argo perform, and she was determined that they should at least get a glimpse of this once-wild stallion that they had fallen in love with over the past nine months.

Her theme song 'Men in Black' by The Canz was remarkably fitting in the circumstances and the lyrics suited Vicki and Argo to perfection. Dressed in a rugby shirt, and with the silver fern painted on Argo's rump, they made a striking picture as they entered the ring. Holding her injured arm against her body and unable even to hold the Silver Fern flag as she'd planned, Vicki slowly guided Argo around the arena.

Like they'd practised only hours before, Argo stepped up onto the moving trailer and stood while it was driven the length of the arena. When it stopped, he turned and got off. Since it was all done at a walk,

TOP
Argo balancing on a moving trailer during his Stallion Makeover of the Year freestyle.

BOTTOM
Vicki and Argo are presented with a rug for winning Fan Favourite.

Top
The collage Amanda made in the lead up to Horse of the Year to help
her visualise competing successfully in the Olympic Cup.

Bottom
Amanda and Cassanova competing in the Olympic Cup.

this was easy enough for Vicki to pull off. She asked Argo to trot, and they then did some basic flatwork, but as Vicki rode past us her face was white with pain and we were really worried. She had just a few minutes left before she could dismount, but she needed to hold herself together for a little longer. Picking up to a canter, she turned Argo and jumped the goal posts before halting and asking him to rear; they had completed only a fraction of their workout, but it was more than anyone could have thought possible with just one arm, and Argo had looked after Vicki every step of the way. As he rose up on his hind legs the roar from the crowd was deafening. Everyone had seen Vicki fall only an hour before and no one had expected her to return to the arena to compete again.

Thirty minutes later the horses returned to the arena for the last element of the Stallion Makeover final: the timed obstacle course. By now the pain was at its worst and the effects of the pain-killers had well and truly worn off. It took everything Vicki had to get Argo around the course one-handed, but they finished with the third fastest time out of the eight combinations. The Stallion Makeover of the Year was now complete, and Vicki joined the line-up to wait for the final placings to be announced. Vicki and Argo were called forward as the winner of Best Conditioned, which had been scored during the Trot Up days earlier, and to Vicki's shock she was also crowned Fan Favourite. The voting had been open for months leading up to the final competition, and Argo had obviously won the hearts of the people with his noble and proud bearing.

The overall placings in the Stallion Makeover Final were then announced, and even with a significantly simplified workout Argo finished in fourth place. Most of what Vicki had trained him to do over the past 10 months had been wasted on the night — the most impressive thing she'd managed to pull off one-handed was riding up onto the moving vehicle, something the horse had learnt just hours earlier — but it had still been enough to rank him as one of the leading horses.

The top three placings were then announced, with Tina and Rock Star the overall champions. Their liberty performance, both on the ground and ridden, had been breathtaking to watch and they were very worthy winners. In fact, every horse in the Stallion Makeover was at an extremely high standard, and watching them perform was one of the most moving things I had ever seen. The Kaimanawa stallions had proved beyond a shadow of a doubt that not only were they were worth saving from slaughter, but that they could thrive in domestication.

THE HORSE OF THE YEAR WASN'T QUITE OVER for us, though; Amanda still had her most important class of the weekend, the Olympic Cup. At the ring Amanda had a huge support base. As well as Vicki, she had the help of friends and fellow competitors, Sally and Phillip Steiner, who had walked the course with her and were assisting in the warm-up arena.

When she entered the ring she looked around at the imposing jumps without fear; she had been practising for this moment for more than a year. Jump after jump, she and Cassanova cantered around the 1.50–1.60-metre course. When they passed through the finish flags, they were faultless: the first combination to do so.

Although only four combinations jumped clear, any horse that had completed the course in 12 faults or less was called back to compete in the second round, carrying their score with them. It was a huge advantage for Amanda to start with a score of zero. She was the youngest of the four competitors sitting in first-equal position. With $40,000 on offer to the winner, there was huge pressure. While the course was changed and the jumps raised in height, Phillip kept Amanda focused.

They soon returned for the second round and Cassanova jumped strongly, although he dropped two rails. This dropped them to fifth-equal placing, alongside living legends Maurice Beatson and his veteran showjumper My Gollywog, who had won the class previously.

Cassanova and My Gollywog were the only New Zealand-bred horses in the line-up; the top four place getters had all imported their horses from Europe. It was a remarkable effort for a young combination and Amanda was very proud of Cassanova. Their success gave her great confidence and even bigger ambitions. In the future she hopes to campaign overseas and compete on the European Circuit.

Top
Amanda and Showtym Cassanova competing in the Olympic Cup at Horse of the Year.

Bottom
Amanda and Showtym Cassanova finished fifth in the prestigious class — she was the youngest rider in the line-up and Cassanova the highest-placed New Zealand-bred horse.

EPILOGUE

Lessons learnt

A herd of wild horses in the
Kaimanawa Ranges during the
Kaimanawa Heritage Horses
Ranges Trip in November 2014.

Three years ago we had a dream: to see the wild horses of the Kaimanawa Ranges saved from slaughter. It hasn't been an idle dream, and over the years we have dedicated thousands of hours to raising public awareness, training horses from the musters and coming up with the concept for the Kaimanawa Stallion Challenges, which came to life thanks to the passionate team at Kaimanawa Heritage Horses.

They say that those who are crazy enough to think they can change the world are the ones who do, and after seeing the challenges come to such a stunning conclusion at Horse of the Year we have to agree: if you have enough passion, dedication and vision, anything is possible.

In the months since the muster, the trainers and their stallions have been ambassadors for the breed, winning the hearts of the public just as we had envisioned. Collectively we have achieved more than any one person could accomplish alone, and seeing the grandstands filled to overflowing only highlighted how much things have changed. There was a time, not that long ago, when pre-existing stereotypes overshadowed the true worth of the Kaimanawa horses; the Stallion Challenges have proved to the nation that not only are these horses worthy of living, but they are equal to any other breed.

In an event of this nature there has to be a winner, but for us the results of the Stallion Challenges were not the most important thing; that was never our end goal. Our mission was to save the lives of these horses and transform them into happy and willing partners; in our eyes every one of the Stallion Challenges trainers is a champion and we would like to thank them all for joining us on this journey to inspire a new generation to love our wild horses.

When we first started our work with the Kaimanawas we could never have imagined the journey it would take us on. While there is no way we could have arrived where we are today on purpose, with life having shaped us and circumstances having guided us on a path not necessarily of our choosing, we wouldn't change a thing. We never planned to tame wild horses, write books, film documentaries or have a reality television show based on our work, but I don't think that these talents were given to us by chance. The things we are passionate about are not random; they are our calling, and we know that with influence comes great responsibility. We are not here for the fame, we are here for the good of the horses, and we hope that our vulnerability and honesty inspires positive change for thousands more horses, both wild and domesticated.

It seems surreal when people ask for our autographs, or even that they look up to us, because in our eyes we are ordinary humans; it's incredibly humbling to receive such recognition for our work. The highest honours we have ever received perhaps come from our horses themselves: we count ourselves blessed that they allow us into their lives and place their trust in us, and we are careful not to take this for granted.

Like the Kaimanawas, we are battle-scarred, imperfect and fundamentally unique. These wild horses, which are entrusted into our care, are our most honest critics and most valued teachers, and every one has had their own lesson to teach us. Argo embodies the true definition of equine genius and has left us speechless at just how fast a horse can learn; if he were human he would be a child scholar, and we continue to be astounded at his ability to learn something after only being shown how to do it once.

DOC and Hoff reinforced our belief that horses are never difficult without cause, and helped us to gain a better understanding of horses that suffer from both physical and emotional issues. While we strived to do everything possible to help them, both were too far gone to have any quality of life in domestication, and we had to look deep within ourselves to decide what was in each horse's best interests. They also taught us that life in the wild is not an ideal existence and proved, beyond a shadow of a doubt, that hoof, teeth and skeletal issues are rampant in wild horses. Both would have suffered from slow and painful deaths without human intervention.

Nikau taught us the importance of purpose and heart; he has never been a hard worker or enjoyed arena work, and identifying his strengths and working with them involved a huge learning curve. Although he showed talent for top-level jumping he lacked the heart for it, so Amanda focused on what he enjoyed — hacking out over the hills, swimming in the river and cantering down the beach. We could have undoubtedly moulded him into a competition prospect, but we didn't save him from slaughter only to subject him to a life of resignation.

Elder has shown us the true meaning of grace and perseverance: true patience is not the ability to wait but how we act while we wait. I have spent hundreds of hours with him since the muster and, although I don't understand why he is taking so long to adapt, I am in awe of his proud and gentle soul. Every day he walks up to eat grass out of my hand and he will follow me anywhere, but still he avoids direct human contact. I know that he likes me and that our trust in each other is mutual, but Elder is a work in progress. He has many more lessons to teach me in the upcoming years and I feel that our journey is only just beginning.

Other horses teach us in more personal ways — they are a part of our own journey of self-discovery and change the very fabric of our identity.

Anzac taught me the power of self-belief, and with him I achieved more than I could have dreamed. Whenever I doubted my ability to train a wild stallion, he affirmed that I was doing something right, and I desperately needed to know that. Watching Anzac develop into a happy, fun-loving pony has been my greatest equestrian accomplishment, and I am hugely thankful for everything he has given me.

OUR JOURNEY WITH WILD HORSES is only just beginning and we can only imagine what the future holds. As I write, we are just a few weeks from flying out to America to spend 100 days taming wild Mustangs. Two million wild horses used to roam the Wild West, but now just 32,000 can be found on public land. Unlike New Zealand, in America the captured Mustangs are stockpiled in government holding facilities, and there are currently more than 50,000 horses languishing in these prison-like environments due to a lack of people willing to re-home them. It's a far from ideal existence for these once-wild horses and we hope that our journey with the Mustangs can inspire positive change.

ACKNOWLEDGEMENTS

Thank you

A HUGE THANK YOU TO EVERYONE who made the Kaimanawa Stallion Challenges a success; the end result was far more than we could have ever hoped for, dreamed or imagined. Not only did you guarantee the survival of the stallions competing, but you have hopefully ensured that Kaimanawas will have the respect and love of many generations to come — not only saving the lives of the Stallion Challenges horses, but Kaimanawas from future musters as well.

To the trainers, thank you for opening up your homes and your hearts to the wild stallions you saved — they quite literally owe you their lives. Even bigger thanks goes to the sponsors — CopRice, Thoroughbred Floats, WashBar, Saddlery Warehouse, John Wilson Sculptures, Horse Gifts and TuffRock. Without your passionate support the events wouldn't have attracted such high-calibre trainers or had such prestige. To Kaimanawa Heritage Horses, you are an incredible team to work with and I would like to thank you for running with our idea and developing the Stallion Challenges into one of the most inspiring displays of horsemanship that this nation has ever seen. To the public, thank you for embracing the challenges, attending the events and falling in love with our nation's wild horses; they need you, and I am so appreciative that they are gaining the recognition they so justly deserve.

Perhaps the greatest acknowledgement should go to the horses themselves; to all the Kaimanawas that have adjusted to domestication — especially the Stallion Challenges horses — I admire your ability to embrace change and thank you for allowing us into your lives.

To the film crew that worked with us on the television series *Keeping up with the Kaimanawas*, you were a pleasure to work with and we loved every minute of it. A special thanks to Rob for pulling together such an amazing and talented crew, and especially to Dean (our primary cameraman) and Esta (our director), who spent most of the five months after the muster filming us training the horses. Having cameras following us around could have been a painful experience, but you both made it an adventure that we thoroughly enjoyed. We feel very fortunate to have you on our team; you have become close friends and we value you more than you know.

To my family, I am so proud of all of you and I love how the wild horses bring us together to work as a team. Mum, you are invaluable in all that you do; thank you for always being there for us. Dad, I am so proud of the horseshoe sculptures you are creating and I would like to thank you for donating the life-sized rearing stallion to the winner of the Stallion Makeover final. It means the world to us that you support our work with the wild horses. To my older sister, Vicki, you are one of the bravest and most talented people I know; every time I watch you work with horses I learn something new. Thank you for sharing your knowledge and empathy with others. To my little sister, Amanda, thank you for being exactly the person you are; you have already achieved so much in your short life and I know it's only the beginning for you. Your humour, positive outlook on life and ability to dream big are inspirational; thank you for challenging and encouraging me.

To my friends, thank you for always being there for me and making me a better person; I wouldn't want to do life without you. A special thanks to Sarah, Alexa, Kirsty, Kalindi and Connie for holding me accountable and listening to this story during the editing process — this book wouldn't have been written without your constant bribes and encouragements!

To my team at Penguin Random House — Alex, Teresa, Debra, Sam and Stuart — thank you for your ongoing support; it's been a pleasure working with you all. Thank you for believing in me and giving me the creative freedom to document our work with the wild horses. I feel honoured to work with all of you and am excited for what the future holds.